*"**More Than a Paycheck** is a Wonderfully Insightful book that I know will help many couples in these turbulent financial times. The heartfelt, examples you shared brought laughter and tears but always ended with the HOPE that one can always have in knowing Jesus and learning to trust HIM in ALL things. I was encouraged by every story and compelled to put into practice some of the steps you have outlined to regain financial freedom and maintain it. Thanks so much for birthing this work out by the Spirit (HE is the best teacher ever) and for sharing your life experiences so transparently, and giving us tools of wisdom to re-establish financial balance and yet keep our marriage relationships vital! Bless you, Sharon!"*

Fay Bonds
Elder, Living Waters Cathedral COGIC
Waukegan, IL

***

D1253926

"My Dear Sharon Almon has written a must-read primer for anyone considering marriage or is married. From my observation of Sharon and her husband, they are a perfect portrait of a Godly marriage and relationship. In every possible way, they show their love, respect and value for one another; the love of Jesus personified.

Sharon is a prototype of not only a wonderful wife, but also the epitome of femininity. Read this book and learn from one of God's sweetest and best wife, mother, sister, church member walking on earth!"

First Lady Mary A. Jackson
Word In Action Fellowship Church
Atlanta, GA

***

"This book reminds me of a well written novel...the author pulls you in and you don't want to put it down. It does not matter if you are single, engaged or married; I believe this book offers something for everyone! You will be carried away on a wonderful journey of true love...a must read"

Barbara P. Mayfield
Managing Director
Priority One Health Care Professionals
Stone Mountain, GA

***

"The author did an amazing job at assimilating valuable life changing financial/budgeting information while keeping the reader totally engaged...a real page turner. This book is a must read for every household!"

Pastor Michelle Jones
Living Waters Cathedral COGIC
Waukegan, IL

***

MORE THAN A PAYCHECK

A WIFE'S STORY OF FAITH, LOVE
AND RENEWAL IN THE FACE OF
FINANCIAL ADVERSITY

More Than A Paycheck

A wife's story of faith,
love and renewal
In the face of financial adversity

Sharon L. Almon

Unless otherwise indicated, all scripture quotations are from the King James Version of the Bible.

More Than A Paycheck
Published by:
Sharon Almon
Stone Mountain, GA

ISBN 978-0-9980168-0-1 (print book)
ISBN 978-0-9980168-1-8 (eBook)

Copyright © 2017 by Sharon Almon
All rights reserved.

No part of this book may be used or reproduced in any manner whatsoever without written permission of the author.

Cover Design by Shrawan Kumar

Printed in the United States of America

DEDICATION

I would like to take this opportunity to dedicate this book to my husband Maurice; my parents the late Preston and Lucille Barrett and to my children James and Christine.

First my husband: Maurice affectionately known as "Sweet Reese" has been the love of my life for over 35 years. He initiated and inspired me to write our story from a wife's point of view. He encouraged me to be transparent regarding a very intimate subject. How his unforeseen job loss three times over a ten year period impacted our relationship and marriage. Even when I was not sure, he kept saying, "honey your story could help other wives going through the same challenge". His faith in God, belief in me and his commitment to our marriage and family has helped to see our family through some difficult days. Thank you for your unconditional love and support in completing this project.

Second my parents: They both transitioned into their heavenly home and are resting side-by-side; my dad November 16, 1977 when I was just 17 years old and mom more recent on April 3, 2016. There are absolutely no words in the English language to express my gratitude for their love, sacrifice and mentorship. Although my time with my dad was brief on earth he taught me so many valuable life lessons regarding work ethic and how a couple should work together in managing a household. My mom will be my queen forever. She helped me to complete chapter two "What My Parents Taught Me" before her transition. Her attention to dates and detail helped to shape my story and reflects who I am as a woman today. She was so excited that I was working on this project. Although they are no longer physically here, in my heart I know they would be pleased. I am so very grateful for the beautiful loving marriage they lived before me. Their legacy will live forever within me and for generations to come!

Finally my two wonderful children: James and Christine I am so very proud and thankful for the adults you have become. When I shared the project with you both, you immediately believed in me. Your love and support kept me going, even when I wanted to procrastinate and give up. I did not want to let you down. I love you both dearly.

***

ACKNOWLEDGEMENTS

First, I would like to acknowledge my Lord and Savior Jesus Christ. His love, joy, peace and provisions strengthened me during some extremely difficult days, as we navigated through our financial storm. I am convinced that I am living out my purpose through sharing our story.

To Barbara and Floyd Mayfield, my loving sister and her husband: Barbara, as long as I can remember you have been my role model. Before you were married and now, after 44 years of marriage to your sweetheart, your relationship is still flourishing. You both have been there for us during some difficult days. Your continued prayers, taking us out to dinner, paying it forward to entertainment events and placing monetary gifts in a card just because…Thank you for your love and support it will never be forgotten.

To my special niece Michelle and her husband Paul Jones, pastors of Living Waters Cathedral. I love you to the moon and back. You will always be my little sister and I am so grateful to see the beautiful woman, wife and mother you are today!

To all of my siblings: Preston, Brenda, Barbara, Donald, Ike, David, Joe and (Carliss & Stella deceased). I love you dearly. Chapter 2 was co-authored by mom before her transition and I know it will hold a special place in your heart.

Sincere appreciation goes to my visionary and leader Bishop Wiley Jackson and First Lady Mary Jackson. Your marriage of over 24 years is a beautiful example of God's love on earth. Bishop, thank you and first lady for your servants' heart and entrusting us to serve as coordinators of the marriage ministry for over 10 years.

Our marriage ministry committee you rock! - Ron and Gloria Johnson, James and Jana Duncan, Geff and Sally Nelson and Arnold and Mary Goodson. Love you dearly

Dr. Venessa A. Brown, thank you for your ongoing support and for taking the time to contribute. You are one of my biggest cheerleaders!

Fay Bonds, Denise White, Tricia Middleton, Betty Rucker and Paula Bonds a sisterhood forever! Thank you all for a listening ear, shoulder to cry on and laugh on. You are the best and truly nothing but death can ever separate us.

Kimberly Ivory Graves: You have been an absolute Godsend. I appreciate you more than you will ever know. Your insight and guidance has been extremely helpful.

A special shout out to the individuals who agreed to participate in the interviews. Your willingness to share your brief stories will provide real life insight how you overcame financial adversity.

Charlotte and Dan Hayes, Spring of Life Couples Ministries: Eric and Nancy Montano, the partnerships have been wonderful.

Don and Denise Showell: You have championed all of our marriage efforts from Day 1.

John and Monica Pearson thank you for all of your continued prayers, love and support.

Sally and Ken Trager thank you for over 30+ years of friendship!

To everyone who will purchase this book, thank you in advance for your support. May our love story of triumph inspire you to invest in your marriage. The long range dividends are worth it all!

***

TABLE OF CONTENTS

Dedication   vii

Acknowledgements   xi

Foreword   ixx

Introduction   xxiii

CHAPTER 1

The Three Keys - Faith, Friendship and Fun   1

CHAPTER 2

Things My Parents Taught Me   7

CHAPTER 3

Partner for Life   15

CHAPTER 4

Friendship to Courtship   23

CHAPTER 5

The Early Years   37

CHAPTER 6

Building Our Faith, Family and Finances   47

CHAPTER 7

Life In Transition   69

CHAPTER 8

The "Peach" State of Mind   83

CHAPTER 9

Living A Downsized Life   93

CHAPTER 10

He's Worth What???   111

CHAPTER 11

Business As Usual? Not…   117

CHAPTER 12

Bringing Home the Bacon   125

CHAPTER 13

Talk to Me   143

CHAPTER 14

My Hero – I Still Need You   151

CHAPTER 15

Cheerleader   157

CHAPTER 16

Re-tooling the Romance   163

CHAPTER 17

The Sun Will Shine Again   167

CHAPTER 18

What Are People Saying…Endorsements   175

About The Author   181

FOREWORD

It was in January of 1980 at Greenville College that I met Sharon L. (Barrett) Almon, one of the few friends my mother told me I would be able to count on one hand in my lifetime. Sharon has been one of those five lifetime friends that allow me to never forget the winter of 1980. Our friendship has blossomed over the years to a sisterhood and a mutual respect for each other. When we first met we were second semester freshmen; she would invite me to her room, boss me around, and give me lots of great baked goods. But more than anything, during those moments when we would eat snacks, laugh, cry, and chat just about everything, I knew we would be lifetime friends. Sharon has always been very direct, honest, helpful and independent. We share those personal characteristics and are able to laugh and cry together and live in our truths. I was Sharon's spy in college, and we loved laughing about all of the things I would discover and bring back to what I called our own "chat room." Today, we still meet at Red Lobster at least two to three times per year to chat, cry, and laugh about our lives and the people we love.

More Than A Paycheck, in my opinion, is a story of unconditional love and true soul mates. Sharon's ability to make a way out of no way is without question a courageous task. Her foundation in the Lord, and love and respect for Reese allowed her to reflect on what matters, and the value of maintaining a sense of "oneness" while getting through hard times. *More Than A Paycheck* is about a marriage grounded in faith, love for God, family, fun, and true commitment to each other.

I have followed Sharon's career since we left college, and her work on behalf of families, children, and her church community as a whole has without question highlighted her commitment to mankind and making the world a better place. She has treated people with the same dignity and respect she has for her own family and children. ***More Than A Paycheck*** is definitely in line with her commitment to transparency, marriage, love, family and friendship. I will be forever grateful that Sharon asked me to write the foreword for her first book. A story of loyalty, living, loving and learning, this book will be invaluable for couples who have to make hard choices in their marriage; for couples who are searching for strategies to stay together; for couples who are searching to become friends; for couples who want to find their way back to mutual respect for each other; for couples who need to forgive each other; for couples who have not had fun in a long time; for couples who need to laugh with and at each other; and more importantly, for individuals who are about to make that leap of faith to become a couple.

Thank you, Sharon and Reese, for being great examples of what commitment looks like, and what it means to embody the words of Robert Schuller: "Tough times never last, but tough people do." Sharon, thanks for being a change-agent, and for finding the courage to share your story, that others might see the rainbow that you saw on your wedding day!

Sisters for Life,

Dr. Venessa A. Brown
Associate Chancellor
Office of Institutional Diversity and Inclusion
Affectionately: Sweet V
St. Louis, MO

***

INTRODUCTION

My college sweetheart and husband of 35 years and I thought we were living the American dream; if there is such a thing! We both attended college earning our degrees through dedication and hard work, paying for tuition through grants, college work study and yes, student loans. We borrowed collectively $20,000. In the 80's that seemed like a ton of money but we worked hard and paid every penny back, both bank and government federal loans. By 2003 we purchased our third home and the only debt we had was our mortgage! We were absolutely ecstatic and life was good. Being a couple of faith tithed 10% of our income to our place of worship, gave to several charitable organizations annually including our college Alma Mater and donated clothing each year to a non-for-profit organization. We saved 10% or more of our income and were doing well in our respective careers! We were financially responsible, careful not to extend beyond our financial capability and we lived within our means!

In May of 2003 our world as we knew it would be shaken and changed forever! After 17 years of service as an IT professional at a major insurance company, my husband was downsized as a result of a "restructure". For all of us who lived through this before the economy was in the initial stages of tanking, this was just the beginning! Over the span of 10 years 2003-2013 my husband would be downsized three times! Our marriage, individual roles, communications, intimacy, finances and how we related to one another would be impacted and tested. For the first time in twenty-two years of marriage, I would be the main bread winner and provider for our family of four. Would our marriage get through this? Would we be in survival mode, wounded from the impact of uncertainty, or would we thrive?

I do not profess to be a marriage counselor nor have I spent years collecting statistical data on marriage and what makes marriages work.

Most of my career has been spent in nonprofit management; managing people and resources trusted in my care. I do however feel confident that I can share my story, being transparent in how we kept our marriage strong through difficult economic uncertainty.

Many folks write about experiences after they have successfully come out of a difficult situation or what I call a storm in their life. In looking back over the last 10 years, I kept thinking how wonderful it would have been to have a resource guide or a support team with helpful tools to assist me as I navigated through the unchartered waters.

Going to bookstores is a fun past-time for me and I am especially drawn to the section on relationships and marriage. In most bookstores it is always the same; there are minimal books or self-help resources written on marriage. Certainly none of them truly spoke to sustaining a marriage through difficult and challenging economic times!

Personally I believe marriage rocks!!! It is not the dying dinosaur or negative statistic you always hear or read about in the news. It is an investment like exercise; no pain no gain! Like the stock market dividends, they increase over time. As with a garden you plant a seed but it takes patience and time to reap a harvest. The same goes for a husband and wife relationship over time. The investment will result in a thriving marriage.

The ultimate goal of this book is to provide wives and wives-to-be with tools that can be used to help sustain their marriages through challenging economic times. All of a sudden, by no choice of your own, you may be thrown into the financial leadership role of your home. My hope is that these tools can be applied to whatever your marriage may face. Although this is written to wives and from a wife's perspective, I have included a chapter for husbands on how to relate to your wife if and when this happens and what she needs from you. *(Wives' place this book on his side of the bed with a bookmark on chapter14 exclusively for "Husbands"; put his favorite snack right by the book as an incentive - that snack might be you!!!)*

***

INTRODUCTION

CHAPTER 1

THE THREE KEYS – FAITH, FRIENDSHIP AND FUN

Over the last 35 years I have been asked, "So, What is the Key to your successful thriving marriage?" For me there are three (3) main ingredients: Faith, Friendship and Fun.

First: *"Faith"* - Regardless of who you are there are times in this life you must call upon a higher power or something bigger than yourself to get you through challenging times. My higher power is Jesus Christ. He has guided me through difficult circumstances and I am not ashamed to call him my Lord and Savior. Without his presence I would not have made it. Faith creates the foundation of the relationship and was a place where I could go draw strength when I felt like hopelessness surrounded me. Being a person of faith I wanted to be transparent that my faith system is rooted in Christianity. My prayer is that regardless of what faith you practice or even if you choose not to practice faith, as women we can find common ground. We all need tools to help move us from survival mode to thriving when our spouses have been impacted economically as a result of job loss.

Second: *"Friendship"* - You truly have to "like" a person to survive financial lack over time. My husband is my best friend and there is absolutely no one on this earth that I would rather spend time with than him. His friendship qualities include allowing me to be myself, promoting my individuality. He also has integrity, unconditional love and genuine care for family, friends and community. This of course happened over the 35 years of marriage so investing in our relationship and putting the time in or "work" is an intricate part of developing this friendship.

What might be helpful is to think about how you go about choosing friends? Ask yourself these questions: Who are my best friends? What qualities do they have that attracted me to them and do they accept me unconditionally?

A short list of characteristics you may look for may include: commonality, integrity, trust-worthiness, ability to be one's self, caring for you despite your flaws, and fun to be around. Think about it; would you spend time with your spouse if you were not married to him? Being friends with your spouse and the ability to "like" him will help get you through the difficult times when you don't feel like you even "Love" him.

Third: *"Fun"* - My husband and I always believed in having fun and are advocates of married couple activities. You must do things that add joy to your life each and every day. This is where creativity can come into play. Fun things do not have to be attached to money.

I personally believe some of our best times together include spending less than $25.00. A weekend refresher get-away strengthens the intimacy of your relationship and is of great value when your budget can support this activity. Included in the chapters to follow are several activities that we incorporated in our marriage to keep it fresh, exciting, interesting and attractive sexually! Yes, I said sexually. This is an area that can suffer when there are financial deficiencies in a relationship and if not addressed could ultimately leave a door open to infidelity.

Faith, friendship and fun are the three main ingredients that have guided our marriage through sunny days and through times of storm. This is how we live out our relationship on a day-to-day basis.

Remember a marriage has peaks and valleys that can be compared to a weather forecast. There will be days that are sunny, stormy, hot, cold, windy, a tornado, a hurricane and yes even a tsunami. Each forecast brings its beauty and its challenges but my faith does know "no storm" lasts forever. With the right tools and resources you can get through anything life may bring, not surviving but thriving!

MORE THAN A PAYCHECK

CHAPTER 2

THINGS MY PARENTS TAUGHT ME

I am the youngest child and daughter of ten children, five girls and five boys. The foundation of our past shapes our framework in how we interact with others, respond to challenges, approach love and view finances. Certainly without a doubt my parents were my role models and without their love and guidance, I would not be the woman I am today.

Both of my parents were born in the South. My dad was born in Rome, Georgia August 28, 1919. He left high school after completing 9th grade to pursue his love as a professional tap dancer. This was his life for nine years and he used his earnings to help support his mom and sister. When I was a little girl my dad would tap dance in the kitchen, showing us a few dance moves of his former life. It was exciting to see him perform just for us. He was written up in the Chicago, Illinois Defender Newspaper as the young man with the educated feet. He would tap dance on china plates without breaking them. One of his career highlights included being the opening act in night clubs on Beale Street in Memphis, Tennessee with legend greats such as Nat King Cole and Louis Armstrong. He left the nightclub scene after nine years to become a full time Evangelist and for a brief period he pastored a church in the Pentecostal movement in which I was raised.

My dad passed away November 16, 1977 at the age of 58 and although I was only 17 when he died, my ideas of the most important characteristics in a man were already formed. He was active with me in Indian Guides and Princess, a program of the Young Men's Christian Association (YMCA) which gives opportunity for daughters and fathers to bond.

He took me fishing and camping at Eagle Lake in Racine, Wisconsin and yes I baited my hook with worms, minnows and a Wheaties mixture he made for catching Carp fish with my cane pole. I was a daddy's little girl for sure!

Sitting on his lap giving him hugs and kisses when he would return home from speaking engagements was part of our father daughter ritual. I would feel so special when given the opportunity to travel with him especially when he would introduce me to the visiting congregation prior to speaking.

My dad exemplified his love and faith in putting God first in his life. He treated mom like a queen, bringing her flowers and candy just because... His strong work ethic and integrity were demonstrated by working three jobs just to make sure we had the basic needs met. This included a home to live in, food to eat, clothing to wear and most of all love. He also lived by faith that God's principles would work. He was the standard I would use to measure every young man that would come into my life and ultimately how I said "Yes" to my husband of 35 years!

My mom was born in Yazoo City, Mississippi May 12, 1923 and she was a sharecropper's daughter who chopped cotton in the spring and picked cotton in the fall. She worked from sun up to sun down, 13 hour shifts earning $0.50 each day! Hard to believe in today's economy but true. She worked in the cotton fields for 10 years of her life. The hard work in the cotton fields shaped her work ethic.

She later attended a private high school in Lexington, Mississippi earning her High School Diploma. This was a great accomplishment because her dad only completed 3rd grade and her mom completed 6th grade. She was the first to graduate high school in a family of 13 children. After high school and at the age of 21 she made a conscious decision not to farm any longer. She purchased a one-way ticket to Chicago, Illinois on a Greyhound bus. Seated in the rear behind the black curtain dividing the African Americans then called Negroes from the Whites was her reality. The word "Colored" was posted on every public bathroom, water fountain, restaurant, and movie theater, but this never diminished her self-worth or confidence in who she was as a person.

Her faith in God, strength, and determination inspired her to believe there had to be a better way of living.

My parents met in Chicago, Illinois during a church service and were married July 11, 1947. Their loving relationship and journey of 30 years together experienced peaks and valleys. They remained committed to God and each other but the first seven years of marriage were impacted by financial challenges. According to mom, she did not go into the workforce full time until I turned age four. It just was not cost effective to have childcare for so many children. Having such a large family and living off the minimal salary of my dad was difficult.

In those days, couples, especially in the Pentecostal movement, did not practice many birth control methods. In my case it was a blessing as I may not have existed since I am the youngest of ten children!

I have fond memories of going camping, picking vegetables on a farm in Wadsworth, Illinois, fishing in Wisconsin and storing fish for the winter in our freezer. I observed mom making homemade jelly, yeast rolls, and apple cobbler.

Many of these activities were done out of necessity but while I was growing up, it was just fun and the memories created were memories I wanted to create and replicate when I had a family. In the early years we may have been categorized as poor by the poverty guidelines of the United States Government but we were rich in love. Mom shared that by the time the last three children were born, finances were much better. We were living in a middle class community in a home filled with love and sacrifice.

Dad secured a good job in janitorial services at a pharmaceutical company and mom retired from a government job after 22 years of service. Their faith in God, determination, strong work ethic and never looking for a hand out but a hand up instilled values in me that sustain me today. They lived the American dream as they knew it by creating a nurturing, loving environment and showing me that money is a tool that I managed. Money does not manage me! Their mentorship instilled qualities in me that established my priorities: God first, treat others the way I want to be treated, and be a good steward over all that is entrusted to me, my marriage, children, career and finances.

These attributes helped me to survive some of my darkest days during our economic uncertainty. My parents' example of how they responded to financial challenges would be a catalyst and reservoir I could draw from in my own marriage.

***

CHAPTER 3

PARTNER FOR LIFE

Can you think back to where you were? What you were wearing? and who you were with when you met your partner for life? Regardless if you have been married one year or fifty years, there is something very special about that first encounter.

I actually met my husband twice, once when I was a senior in high school at the age of 17 and then again a year later. It is so hilarious when I think about it now. It truly was predestined for us to be together and divine destiny that brought us together as both of us were dating other people when we met. In reflection I realize our plans may not always be God's best for our lives.

It was the spring of 1978 on the campus of Greenville College, a 4-year private liberal arts institution with under 1,000 students in enrollment. The school was in a small quaint little town that reminded me of the fictitious town of Mayberry.

Baby boomers can surely relate to the Andy Griffith Show with Andy Taylor, Barney Fife, Aunt Bee and Opie Taylor who represented a town of people who cherished values and did the right thing. At that particular time the highlight of residing in Greenville, Illinois was going to the Dairy Queen. Crime was minimal to non-existent and folks rarely locked their doors at night. It was almost "utopia", a community that possessed near perfect qualities. It is quite different today and there is much more infrastructure surrounding the college and campus; and yes, I am sure folks are locking their doors. My interest in attending the college was the excellent academic success rate, the faculty student ratio and that it was Christ centered.

It was my senior year in high school when a friend and I purchased round trip tickets to Greenville College located in Greenville, Illinois. Greenville is approximately an hour east of St. Louis, Missouri. We had taken the Greyhound bus over six hours to spend a few days on campus to decide if I wanted to attend in the fall of 1978.

With the exception of the baseball team, a few campus tour guides and those International students too far from home to make the trip, most of the students had left campus to enjoy spring break. Earlier during the day we saw a portion of the baseball team in the dining commons huddled together eating lunch and proudly displaying their

Greenville College Panther baseball uniforms and jackets.

As we explored the beautiful landscaped campus we noticed one of the players slowly walking in our direction.

He was tall and thin with a friendly demeanor. As he approached he stopped and greeted each of us respectfully. We did a little small chit chat shared that we were from Waukegan, Illinois (suburban girls). He shared he was from Chicago, Illinois (City slicker). We were being careful not to share too much. He was warm, kind and extended his personal tour guide services to us during our visit.

He stated, "If you need anything please let me know, I will be happy to show you around or answer any questions you may have". When he walked away and we knew he could no longer hear us we turned to each other and laughed. I said to my friend, "sure he would like to show us around".

We both were thinking was he being kind or just flirtatious. At that particular time I had a boyfriend at home who I cared about deeply so looking at another guy was out of the question or so I thought!

After I returned home I discussed my college campus visit with my mom. She was very supportive of whatever decision I was going to make. After weighing the pros and cons and given my dad had just passed away in November 1977, I decided it was best to attend a junior college near home and be supportive to my mom for at least another year. So I enrolled in a one year dental program at the College of Lake County in Grayslake, Illinois and graduated in June 1979.

My mom came to me and said, "Sharon you are 18 years old. Why don't you give Greenville College a try"? It did not take long for me to send in my application, receive my acceptance and off to Greenville College I went!

When I arrived on Greenville College campus in August of 1979 for freshman orientation, I was excited and ready to achieve in every area of my life! I had absolutely no idea I would meet my best friend, lover, provider and partner for life because in my mind I already had met him. The year I left for Greenville College, my current boyfriend left for a Historically Black College and University (HBCU) in the South. We had made an agreement that if this relationship was meant to be after graduation from college, we would probably get married. I was not pre-engaged but it was just an understanding we had. He had always treated me respectfully, had wonderful character and I knew he had long term relationship potential. We had similar backgrounds. Our families knew each other so it was a perfect scenario.

When I went into the dining commons for the very first time after arriving on campus the very first person I saw was the tall thin baseball player. (My husband is 6'4) I said to my roommate "Look at that guy! I met him in 1978 when I initially visited Greenville College and he is still here"! This was the second time I met this tall baseball player. What role would he play in my life and why?

MORE THAN A PAYCHECK

CHAPTER 4

FRIENDSHIP TO COURTSHIP

As I previously stated I initially met my current husband affectionately called Reese in the spring of 1978 during my visit to Greenville College. Then I reconnected with him a year later in 1979 in the fall of my freshmen year.

On both occasions it was a strictly meet and greet as we both were dating individuals who attended other universities.

Greenville College demographics in 1979 were comprised primarily of Caucasian students who made up the majority on campus. There may have been 50 African Americans and a few International students which made up the minorities. As a result the African American students became a close knit community and I quickly became familiar with the males and females on campus.

There were also platforms such as Rapport and Reverence that promoted and brought awareness of minority concerns to the campus. It was through these organizations and sports that Reese and my friendship was birthed and flourished.

Much of our early friendship was spent in groups as he respected my relationship with my boyfriend and I respected the relationship he had with his girlfriend. Neither of us ever wanted to cross the line.

To tell you the truth I loved being in his presence because it was refreshing knowing I could spend alone time with him and trust his character. I never experienced a male/female relationship where there was no outside agenda or expectations.

This was refreshing that men and women could be "just friends" or shall I say, for a while!

Everyone on campus both male and female along with the faculty and administration seemed to respect him. He was friendly, funny, kind and they called him "Sweet Reese". Remember he had already been on campus for a full academic year before I arrived. He was always the consummate gentlemen and I wondered if that was truly him or a strategy to eventually win my heart over!

I actually remember writing my boyfriend and sharing with him that I had met this nice guy and his name was Maurice from Chicago, Illinois. I shared how I had been spending a lot of time with him but he is dating someone else as well so it is all good! I did not want any secrets and most of all I wanted a clear conscience.

Most of the time I spent with Maurice was talking about my boyfriend and how much I missed being with him and how I could not wait until Christmas break to see him!

Our friendship grew over the next few months. We would share stories, talk about our classes, participate in the same organizations, laugh together, eat in the dining commons together, meet and watch television and it felt like he was turning into my best friend. There was a trust building that I had not experienced with a young man before because I felt he really saw me. Not the external superficial get dressed up and "look your best on a date me" but the "real me" unedited. He accepted me just as I was with all of my flaws.

Thanksgiving break came quickly. As I left campus and went home for the week, I felt something was missing. I was aware that Maurice went to see his girlfriend for Thanksgiving break. She attended a University less than an hour away from our campus. My boyfriend would not be coming home for Thanksgiving because of the distance but I would see him Christmas break and was excited about our reunion.

The Turning Point:

Christmas is always an exciting time of the year! It was time to go home and after four months of writing letters, sending cards, and telephone calls my boyfriend would be picking me up from the Union Train Station in Chicago, Illinois.

I arrived in Chicago and there he was my boyfriend looking dapper and handsome as I remembered. He slowly walked toward me and we embraced.

Not a prolonged hug but it felt like he missed me too. He gathered my luggage and off to Waukegan we went talking about our respective college experiences. He lined up tickets for us to attend a college basketball game.

We enjoyed a double date with my brother and while in the car talking with my boyfriend I actually called him Maurice. I chalked it up to me spending so much time with Maurice on campus and nothing more. We went on a few other dates before returning to our respective schools. It seemed our relationship was on track and all was good but in the back of my mind, I thought of my friendship with Maurice.

The Greenville College baseball team had gone to Texas for Christmas break and Maurice, who played pitcher, was on the road trip. I was not sure if he was thinking of me but I certainly thought about him and I missed our daily conversations.

During the final days of the Christmas break, Maurice called me from Texas and when I answered the phone and heard his voice, I actually lit up like a Christmas Tree! I shrieked with joy and wanted to hear all about the tournament and what he was doing. He told me he missed our talks and most of all he missed me. When the called ended I knew he was the one. This was my turning point and I knew my relationship with my boyfriend would have to be severed. You may be saying, "You knew he was the one after one call???" The answer to that question is "Yes".

I knew in my heart from the way he made me feel just hearing his voice. It revealed to me that a friendship and foundation had been built over the last several months and I never wanted to be out of his presence again. This was an authentic person who may only come once in a lifetime. He was someone I could trust who cared for me unconditionally. This friendship was the foundation that gave me hope that we could have a future together. It was blind faith but I was willing to take a leap knowing there still was another hurdle...his girlfriend.

Knowing my feelings had changed, I shared with my boyfriend shortly after returning to campus that I thought it best if we go our separate ways. It was only fair to respect the integrity of our relationship and he probably felt we had grown apart as well. We went our separate ways, leaving the relationship with a mutual respect for one another.

The Final Hurdle: His Girlfriend

This is a funny but true story. My sweet loving husband did not find it so funny at the time...Be careful when you write letters at night!!

My boyfriend and I mutually agreed to go our separate ways shortly after Christmas break. Maurice had not officially broken up with his girlfriend. However he communicated to me that was the plan. He wanted to let her down gently. Was I crazy to let go so fast? Were we just friends or did he want to cultivate a long lasting relationship?

It was January of 1980 close to the date of Maurice's 21st birthday. During the winter class break, the majority of the students leave campus, so he was home in Chicago, Illinois. I had to remain on campus with the cheerleading squad to cheer for several basketball games previously scheduled.

One evening, late at night he decided to write two special letters. I was the recipient of one of those letters from Maurice. I read the letter and at the end it said, "Tell your mom hello and I hope her trip to California went well". I knew my mom had not gone to California and realized right away what had happened. You see I always knew about his girlfriend but I am not so sure she knew about me. He wrote two letters that night one to me and one to his girlfriend. I received her letter and she received mine. To this day I have no idea what he said to me in the letter she received. All I can tell you is it was soon after this happened that the relationship between Maurice and his girlfriend ended.

The most embarrassing story is how Maurice's mom shared this epic debacle at his Senior College class picnic in 1982. It was hilarious and everyone laughed until we cried...all but my sweet Maurice!

Our Courtship:

Our courtship officially began my sophomore year and his junior year in college. At that time we were fully engaged into the college life experience and living on campus. I was a Speech Communications major and he was a Business Administration major. In order to earn money toward his tuition he worked for the college in the maintenance department. I still tease him to this day that his maintenance job sealed the deal for me!

When I saw him on that rooftop I knew he would be an excellent provider because there would be nothing he would not do to make an earnest living. He maintained a full academic load, played on the baseball team as a pitcher, participated in the Men of Agora a men's community service fraternity, President of Rapport an organization that brought awareness to minority concerns and sang in the Reverence Choir.

I was busy with a full academic load, basketball cheerleading, a resident assistant, Ladies of Elpinice, a women's community service sorority, Rapport and sang in the Reverence choir.

In spite of our busy college schedules and extracurricular activities we found time to nurture and cultivate our relationship.

I remember our first official date as though it was yesterday. He walked to my dormitory and picked me up at the back stairwell. He had on a blue suit and I wore a beautiful floral dress. He presented me with six carnations in pastel colors with baby breaths and greenery.

We walked a block or two away to Farmers Daughters Restaurant. I ordered the lasagna and he ordered roast beef. We talked for hours and he walked me back to my dorm. He kissed me on the cheek and I floated to my dorm room. He was truly courting me and I loved every minute of it.

We cultivated a wonderful friendship which is a key component to any relationship. I genuinely liked him and loved being in his presence. I could talk to Maurice about any and everything: My joys, sorrows, dreams, fears, including my personal and career aspirations.

During our courtship Maurice also made a personal decision to give his life to Christ. I did not want him to make such a life changing decision to seal the deal on a relationship with me but to do so because that was a lifestyle change he wanted to incorporate in his everyday life. He shared with me how he had observed the way I carried myself on campus and that I truly was different. He wanted that for his own life and I can honestly tell you his personal faith decision has carried throughout every aspect of his life for over 35 years.

After my mom gave her blessing in November of 1980 Maurice asked me to marry him and I said "Yes". He was my knight in shining armor and I was honored to be his partner for life.

CHAPTER 5

THE EARLY YEARS

We were engaged for nine months, just enough time to plan our wedding, get married and return back to our college campus in Greenville, Illinois before classes began late August of 1981. My husband Maurice was going into his senior year and I was going into my junior year. I certainly would not recommend this for everyone but we were in love, mature, and knew divorce was not an option. We were entering a covenant marriage and not a contractual one. Our faith and commitment to each other would guide us through the storms of life.

I was only 20 and my husband to be was 23. We were very young by today's standards and most 20-23 year olds today would not have the tools to deal with the challenges ahead, certainly not the ones we would face.

Our wedding day… "After every dark cloud is a silver lining" is what my mother-in-law whispered in my ear during a rain storm that destroyed our romantic rehearsal dinner. The rehearsal was scheduled to take place at dusk on the beach front of Lake Michigan in the Waukegan, Illinois Harbor. I was not feeling or seeing the rainbow at that specific moment and my nerves were on edge.

One of the ten bridesmaids had to pull out of the wedding the day before due to an unforeseen illness and one of the groomsmen was lost and extremely late for the rehearsal. Needless to say we ended up with over 50 guests in my mother's home for the rehearsal dinner. Not exactly the beach lakefront view!

The next morning, the day of our wedding, I awaken to birds singing, the sun was shining and there was actually a rainbow in the sky! This must be a good sign that today was going to be a wonderful day.

One of my bridesmaids a long time college friend from Colorado, encouraged me to have morning devotions so together we read some positive affirmations and said a calming prayer together. This provided me with comfort and gave me 100% peace.

The entire day was absolutely beautiful we were surrounded by family and friends, especially our new Greenville College friends who loved and supported our decision to walk this journey called life together.

Although my dad could not be there to give me away, I was honored that my oldest brother Preston Barrett Jr., escorted me down the aisle. On August 15, 1981 I married the man of my dreams, my best friend, lover and protector affectionately called "Sweet Reese".

The church was packed to capacity and the wedding went off without a hitch. There were 22 in our wedding party and knowing what I know today I would have reduced that number by 50%. Being young and in college you just wanted all of your friends in the wedding and it was hard to say "no". The thought process was "the more the merrier". I will never forget saying those wedding vows for better or for worse; for richer or for poorer; in sickness and in health, until death do us part…

We took our vows seriously and before we got married we went through a six week intensive marriage workshop at the college we attended. This workshop/seminar covered topics such as communications, finances, family planning, and intimacy. We made an inner vow that "Divorce" was never an option for us.

When we made those vows we had no idea what worse might look like. We just knew our faith and friendship could see us through unchartered waters and so the journey began…

After a five day honeymoon in Lake Geneva, Wisconsin we returned to Greenville College prepared to begin our junior and senior year respectively. We were full-time students, part-time employees both working for the college. Maurice worked in the maintenance department and I worked in the Dean's office and the National Direct Student Loan (NDSL) office. After a brief discussion we decided that I would manage the finances for the family. This was a little comical to me considering he was the business major. However that has been my role in our marriage. Managing finances in a marriage is not gender specific. It is a decision agreed upon between the two of you, who can do it best.

The First two years of our marriage 1981-1983 were spent as full-time students and part-time employees of the college. We were paid monthly so it took careful planning to ensure all bills were paid and accounted for. A monthly budget contributed to our success as a couple. Our income to debt ratio was manageable.

My husband came into the marriage with no credit cards. We jointly secured a Sears credit card together in order to build credit as a married couple. I came into the marriage with one JC Penney credit card in my name. I was careful to pay off monthly balances each month.

Year one of our marriage we rented the first floor of a large farm house owned by one of the college professors. Our rent was only $156.00 per month and included all utilities except our phone bill! What a deal for two bedrooms, one bathroom, a living room, formal dining room, a large eat in kitchen and back porch. Our first year of marriage was shear bliss. We experienced some minimal adjustments but we were so busy getting through college we did not notice anything major. During the second year of our marriage my husband graduated from Greenville College with a B.A. degree in Business Administration. He was extended an offer to work for the college as the night watchman security guard.

He accepted the position and worked third shift which worked for us since I was a student and would sleep while he worked.

I was a senior and selected by the Dean of Housing to be a Hall Director over a freshman dormitory, along with a few houses that female seniors resided. This was a wonderful opportunity for us both as my salary package included: an apartment rent free for a year located in the lower level of the dormitory, dining commons meal cards and a minimal stipend. We lived off the stipend and deposited his monthly income into our savings account.

In 1983 I graduated from Greenville College with a B.A. degree in Speech Communications. I was blessed to achieve a 4.0 GPA both semesters and successfully graduated with Cum Laude Honors. It was an exciting time for our family as I was selected by the College President to give the senior commencement speech. What an honor and memory I will always cherish.

It was time to face the real world and leave the academic comfort of Greenville College campus. I believe these first two years of our marriage set the stage and platform of our relationship and the way we managed our finances. Our goal was to have enough money saved to support our transition once we left Greenville, Illinois. We were financially ready to secure an apartment and live until we found our first jobs post college graduation.

CHAPTER 6

BUILDING OUR FAITH, FAMILY AND FINANCES

It was May of 1983 and after my graduation we relocated to Waukegan, IL a small town situated between Chicago and Milwaukee. This small suburban town was extremely familiar to me because I was born and raised there. My husband was born and raised in Chicago but shared with me he never wanted to raise a family in the inner city so we agreed to move to Waukegan.

My mom resided there along with a few other siblings and relatives which were great comfort to me being newly married. We had not been around family for the first two years of our marriage which is not a bad thing because we only had each other to turn to during challenging times.

Our apartment was move-in-ready as the apartment complex had just been built. It was a beautiful little one bedroom apartment with a lovely club house. It was income based and since we had just graduated from college and both looking for jobs our monthly rent was adjusted accordingly.

During our first two years of marriage the home and apartment we lived in were fully furnished. Our new apartment would need furniture so I took the liberty to go to Waukegan, Illinois during my spring break and purchase furniture from what they now call "sheik" consignment shops; back then they were called second hand used furniture stores. Call them what you like, I walked away with a box spring, mattress, two dressers, two end tables, four lamps and one cocktail table all for under $200.00. The kitchen furniture was given to us by my father-in-law; so we were all set. Thankfully my mom graciously stored all of the items in her garage until we returned in May 1983.

Storage units were not popular at this time plus this was an additional savings, no cost rental space a win-win for us and our limited budget. I was a mean negotiator with salesmen and still negotiate prices today! We were determined to live within our means. Our motto was cash and carry. If we did not have the cash to purchase an item it remained in the store.

Building Faith:

Over the next decade and beyond we focused on building our faith which as previously stated is our foundation and cornerstone of every decision we make. Faith would get us through the challenging times we would face throughout our marriage so we could be a testimony to other married couples that they too can succeed.

We are not religious but have a relationship with Jesus Christ who helps to guide our daily life style and decision making. This initially began by us both accepting Him as our Lord and Savior. Think of it as an added bonus or person to guide us through this journey we call life. It is not complicated; it is literally accepting John 3:16 as a biblical principal. *"For God so loved the world that he gave his only begotten son, that whosoever believes in him should not perish, but have ever lasting life."* (KJV) This is a 100% act of faith. There will be times in your marriage that you will face challenges greater than your capability. Finding a place of worship that can speak into your purpose in life is so important.

The ministry that we dedicated our early married and family life to was the Pentecostal church I was born in.

There is no perfect church because as humans we are flawed people. However I can truly say the fundamental foundation, principles and instruction provided, stabilized us as a couple and speaks volumes to our longevity today.

As a couple we attended this small but loving place of worship from 1983–1999. We were dedicated and served in every capacity: youth leaders, praise and worship team members, choir director, deacon, trustee, Easter and Christmas program coordinators, van drivers, vacation Bible school instructors, communion servers and the list goes on and on and on…Whatever was needed we served. We went to church every night of the week except Thursday and sometimes a meeting would be called on Thursday nights.

Looking back I have no idea how we were so active with a young family but we were. We developed friends and relationships we cherish in our hearts today.

During challenging times some folks may turn to other extra marital affairs, alcohol or even drugs; we chose to turn to our faith and faith community for comfort and direction.

Christians are not exempt from hard times but our faith which is strength under pressure would see us through difficulties. Faith is like a muscle in the body that is built and developed over time. Key components of our faith have always included:

1. Sharing our faith with others, not in a condescending way but through our daily lifestyle and in love.

2. Active involvement in a place of worship. This is helpful to gain strength, encouragement and

hear other faith building testimonies from our Pastor and members.

3. Individual and corporate times of devotions and prayer. This is key - just talking to God daily not just when things go bad but just because we love God.

We have always felt our faith has sustained us in every area of our lives and if it worked for other areas why not during economic hard times!

Building Family:

The month of October has proven to be a month of bountiful, beautiful, blessings for our family. I remember it like it was yesterday. We had been married for three years and both were working entry level positions. I was an Estimator Coordinator a fancy name for administrative support at a carton, label and enclosure manufacturer and my husband was an Associate in retail management. We decided jointly it was time to begin our family and it only took about six months for me to conceive. We were absolutely elated.

My husband teases me to this day that both of our children were his "Birthday Babies". Both of our children were conceived in January and my husband's birthday is January 23rd. Not sure if they were birthday babies but I can't argue the fact they were both conceived in January.

Our son and oldest child James Anthony Almon made his grand entry October 20, 1984 at 4:30PM born at Lake Forest Hospital in Lake Forest, Illinois. I had a wonderful pregnancy and very little morning sickness.

His gender was a surprise as it was not routine to do an ultrasound in 1984. The only pregnancy side effect experienced was pregnancy mask. Yes I looked like a sixteen year old with a full blown case of acne. I had never had acne not even in my teens! It was not attractive but to be blessed with a healthy son it was worth it. I worked every day up to the day of his delivery. I went to work Friday, Oct 19th and he was born on the 20th. I remember sending my husband off to work the morning he was born thinking this was our first child and based on what we had read and learned, this could take a while. The Lamaze instructor and doctor communicated to drive to the hospital when the contractions were five minutes apart. So…when I was able to time the contractions five minutes apart I called my husband at work and said, "it's time; come pick me up." Within a few hours after being admitted and responding to questions at the information desk between contractions and breathing, James shot out like a football being tossed across a football field! He made his arrival and when we laid eyes on him we knew that besides loving God and each other we could not love anyone more.

Life was good over the next three years. Raising our son gave us joy we could not have imagined. Career advancement brought financial rewards before our next arrival.

Our daughter and youngest child Christine Ashley Almon made her grand entry almost three years later October 16, 1987 at 8:20AM, also born at Lake Forest Hospital in Lake Forest, Illinois. This was the same day the world watched the rescue of Jessica McClure 18 months old of Midland, TX who had slipped into an 8 inch abandoned well and survived after 58 hours. So this was definitely a day to rejoice not just for the birth of our daughter Christine but for the McClure family as well. This pregnancy was quite the opposite of the first. As with the first pregnancy I worked every day in my new position at a major Healthcare Corporation. I was a customer service representative for the dialysis division and every morning without fail I would visit the women's restroom and regurgitate in real words vomit profusely. Even though I tried to keep things quiet I would hear whispers outside the bathroom door saying, "are you ok?" My response was consistent, "Yes I am great, just pregnant!" Thank God, gratefully the nausea ended after the first trimester and the remaining pregnancy went without incident.

Christine was born using the natural Lamaze method and my husband deserves a medal for his excellent coaching skills. She entered the world the day before family and friends had planned a baby shower in her honor.

My loving husband, the only man at the baby shower, represented me well! When he arrived everyone asked where I was and he responded, "She is not coming. She had the baby yesterday".

Everyone told me he was such a good sport. He sat and opened each gift and with the help of my sisters, made sure the thank you list was detailed with each gift item.

Our family was complete, a son and daughter and our commitment to God and each other was to raise them with faith, love, values, integrity and the ability to give back. We wanted to make certain they received a good education so they could achieve a life far better than our own. Our journey in raising our children included keeping them involved with the youth group at our church and being hands on parents. Both children were enrolled into Cooke Magnet elementary school in Illinois. That exposed them both to the arts, science, sports, dance, violin and orchestra. Most of all they learned the ability to think outside the box and believe anything is possible.

During our children's formative years we made a joint decision for me to leave my corporate position. This decision resulted in my being home for five years to provide them with a great start in life. I can truly say their love for learning, reading books and who they are today is a direct result of the values we instilled early in their development. Are they perfect individuals without flaws? Absolutely not and have they made mistakes most definitely but I can say with all of their flaws and mistakes made we could never be as proud of them as we are today! Life is a journey and in order to achieve there will be pitfalls along the way. It is what you do with those lessons learned that matters. During those five years at home and operating solely on one income helped me to manage and budget the bi-monthly salary my husband made to support a family of four. We kept our spending to the cash and carry concept as we established our household motto in the early years; we managed money, it did not manage us.

I dressed the children at consignment shops and they always looked like a million dollars or at least I thought they did. James our wonderful son has served his country in the United States Navy for over 12 years and is doing extremely well. He has had the opportunity to travel the world and resided in Japan for several years. He was selected to represent the Navy in Antarctica for 45 days during one of his field assignments, laying the groundwork in the field of communications. Our prayer is that through hard work and dedication he will be promoted to the rank of Chief soon.

Christine our beautiful daughter is a 2010 University of Georgia (UGA) graduate. She has worked two jobs since graduation in order to meet her financial responsibilities - layman's terms pay her bills. She momentarily ventured into the field of acting, securing a few non-speaking parts including portrayal of a college student on the House of Payne, a Tyler Perry weekly series. She was in several scenes that aired December 2, 2011 and we were so excited for her. She finally landed a full-time job with a promising career path in Finance and a decent compensation package. We believe in both of our children 100% and know they will create a legacy that honors God and themselves.

Building Finances:

Before we were married we discussed how we would handle our finances.

Our approach to money was that we were stewards and managers over what was entrusted to us through wages earned. Our money would be used as a tool to support the way we lived and to give to others in need. We established a joint bank account, both checking and savings.

I managed the monthly bills and finances and we had ongoing communications to ensure we were on point. Just to be clear, managing the finances did not mean I controlled how the money would be spent. It just meant I had the skill-set to ensure all of the bills were paid on time. This aided in building an excellent credit rating. Money would be set aside for savings, an emergency account would be established and an allowance for each of us would be allocated each week to do as we wished. Our financial principles included:

- Tithes, offerings and not-for-profit giving.
- Savings and investments.
- Fiscal Responsibility -We paid our creditors on time until the debt was paid in full.

Tithes, Offerings and Not-for-profit Giving:

We established a principle that 10% of all we earned would honor God in the form of a tithe. This is a Biblical principle followed in the Bible and can be read in the book of Malachi 3:10 *"Bring ye all of the tithes into the storehouse, that there may be meat in mine house, and prove me now herewith, saith the Lord of hosts, if I will not open you the windows of heaven, and pour you out a blessing, that there shall not be room enough to receive it."* (KJV) This principle has been our covenant since the day we said "I Do" until today. Even through our leanest of times we were consistent in this principle. Some folks would say we couldn't afford to tithe through economic uncertainty but I say we couldn't afford not to tithe. You see honoring God provided prosperity in other areas not just monetary.

Things such as favor in terms of promotions on our jobs, good health, protection for our family, safe travels for our children especially when our son was stationed in Japan for several years these are things money cannot buy. After we give tithes, we also give offerings which are monetary weekly gifts of gratitude to say thank you God for blessing us with an opportunity to earn a living.

These offerings help to advance the good news that Jesus changes lives and support the house of worship. Finally we enjoyed giving to several not-for-profits that are committed to helping families achieve self-sufficiency. This included monetary annual gifts and donations of household goods and clothing.

We operated out of the concept *"to whom much is given much is required"*.

We were not financially rich according to "World" standards but we were rich in love, family and our needs were met.

Savings and Investments:

We tried to save 10% each pay period and more if possible. I personally enjoyed saving and truly like surprising my husband in reaching financial saving goals pre-maturely. I recommend to everyone to save something each pay period. It is not the amount but the consistency that matters even if it is $5.00 per week. That is $260.00 more than you had when you started at the end of the year. We also took advantage of company sponsored 401K, stock, pension plans to establish security for retirement and in case of a financial emergency. I must interject here that it is great and fiscally responsible to do all of the right things in terms of saving and investing but there may come a time in your marriage as did ours that even doing all of the right things are not enough. Even though we had accumulated a substantial savings account it took a supernatural miracle to sustain us.

Fiscally Responsible:

The final component of building finances is being fiscally responsible. The economic turndown for the entire country began in 2007. It began for us in

2003. Prior to this we set a standard in our marriage to be fiscally responsible. When we incurred debt such as our student loans a combined debt of $20K we paid the loan back in full. We were able to finance three homes and a few cars during our marriage securing low interest rates as a result of our excellent credit rating. We have never financed furniture, television sets, clothes etc…these items were always cash and carry or pay within 60 or 90 days and no interest would be charged. Prior to our son going into the Navy he went to college for one year. We paid the tuition for his first year in cash.

Financial experts would probably discourage utilizing savings to pay tuition during economic transition. However we did not want our son to experience student loan debt. Our overall family goal was to live within our means and enjoy the freedom of being debt free. Paying the mortgage in full was the final financial goal. Our day-to-day monthly bills were always paid before or on the due date. We had no idea that our lives would be turned upside down. Beginning in 2003 we would be impacted three times over the next ten years! Would we survive?

MORE THAN A PAYCHECK

CHAPTER 7

LIFE IN TRANSITION

We resided in Waukegan, Illinois from May 1983 until August of 1999. After attending my sister's 25th wedding renewal in 1996 in Stone Mountain, Georgia we contemplated on relocating to the Atlanta metro area.

We simply fell in love with the idea, of living the rest of our natural lives, in a warmer climate, away from the Midwest, and the brutal winters. We also knew if we were going to move, this would be the perfect time. Our son was entering high school and our daughter middle school. As a woman, "security" was rated as one of my top priorities in terms of provisions. So when my husband approached me about relocating from the small town, I knew as home for 39 years, my first response was, "what about our jobs?"

He responded, "I plan to talk with my immediate manager, and Human Resources, to see if I can transfer my current position at the same seniority and pay scale." I did not give the conversation too much thought, because in my heart of hearts, I thought oh well it is a win-win either way. If Human Resources denied the request for transfer, we would remain in Waukegan, Illinois in the second home we had recently remodeled, surrounded by family, friends and our flourishing careers. If the transfer request was approved by his manager and Human Resources we would begin the process of relocating to the Atlanta Metro area: a beautiful area surrounded by mild winters, and an opportunity to build a new life outside of our existing comfort zone.

In approximately a month or so my husband came to me and said I have some news for you. Human Resources approved my husband's request to be transferred to the Atlanta metro area. The real joy was as an IT professional he could work remotely out of our new home.

He only had to return two or three times annually for departmental meetings. All other business could be achieved via conference call.

What a huge savings, no more daily commutes, spending money on lunch, or purchasing business attire. It was like getting an additional salary increase without negotiating.

We gathered the children and shared the news with them. We truly wanted to know how they felt about our family moving to the Atlanta metro area.

They responded excitedly, "Yes let's do it!"

Organization is one of my strengths. So I immediately begin to make a checklist, in order to make the relocation to Georgia a smooth transition. We broke the news to my mom, who was extremely supportive, as well as family and friends who had to get over the initial shock of our leaving our close knit community. Operation relocation went into full court press.

I notified my employer of our decision to relocate at the beginning of April 1999. This gave me approximately four months to assist in the interview process, identify and hire a candidate, and train my replacement since my last day would be the end of July. My position as the Coordinator of the Self-Sufficiency program, for a not-for-profit organization, included assisting single female head of households achieve self-sufficiency through education or entrepreneurship. This was my passion for the last five years. I was committed to seeing lives transformed. Leaving this role would be difficult. During my tenure, I had the opportunity to create various components of the program service delivery process. However growth means change.

Where would we live in Georgia?

My sister, brother-in-law and their two children who were young adults resided in Georgia. Their beautiful home was approximately 20 miles east of Atlanta nestled in a well-designed landscaped community.

We shared our news with them and they were extremely accommodating throughout the entire transition. First, we contacted a realtor online and together we identified homes in our price range.

Virtual tours became our hobby over the course of our long distance home search.

This allowed us to decide if we wanted to view the home during our weekend visit. In May of 1999 we flew down to Georgia with the goal of finding our home within one weekend. Now that I look back the entire relocation was supernatural. Finding a home in three days was quite a challenge.

We walked through at least twenty-five to thirty homes outside of the Atlanta metro area and by Sunday afternoon we had not made one offer.

Exhausted and a little disappointed we said oh well we will just have to schedule another trip down to Georgia.

My brother-in-law said, "Let's do one more drive through the community" as I had fallen in love with their home and its surroundings. The entire area was absolutely beautiful, had wonderful amenities; several tennis courts, pools and surrounded by a man-made lake.

We agreed to go on one more drive through the community. We noticed a house being built on the left side of the street and only the frame of the home and stairwell had been completed. As we stopped the car along the curb and secured the telephone number on the lot sign we decided we had nothing to lose so we called the builder.

He came right over and gave us a walk through the frame of the home. Our imagination had to visualize the space. On the first floor there was a bedroom with a full bathroom. I could see my husband's office with a nice bay window view being in that location. There was also a formal dining room, living room with another bay window, a family room, laundry room and galley styled kitchen.

On the second floor each of our children had their bedrooms, our master bedroom was across the cat walk, and a nice sized bonus room was situated over the garage. The bonus room concept was new to me as we had always had homes with basements in the Midwest.

Even without a basement it was perfect. Four bedrooms and three full bathrooms is what our family of four needed and most important within our price range.

We had already pre-qualified on my husband's salary and with an excellent credit rating we were ready to make an offer.

Although the bank said we qualified to buy a more expensive home our reality was we did not want to exceed living beyond our net pay.

After all we wanted to continue our contributions toward our savings account, buy groceries, and pay our day-to-day living expenses.

This was extremely important given the fact I would no longer be employed during our transitional move.

A Home to Sell:

In all transparency we had a home to sell in Waukegan, Illinois. We communicated to the builder that we could not afford two mortgages and that we must sell our home in Illinois before we could purchase our potential new home in Georgia. Most builders do not like contingencies knowing it is a risk if it takes a long time for a house to sell. He wanted to know how long we thought our home would be on the market. Well...we could not truly answer that but we knew our existing home had been completely remodeled. It was priced to sell, and it had good curb appeal. He said, "you two look like honest people and although two other couples have called and are interested in this home I will allow the contingency for ninety (90) days and then we will have to revisit the contract." We agreed this would be fair and in approximately two hours we signed the contract, paid our earnest money and had to choose everything from the floors to the light fixtures. It was exciting but frightening all at the same time.

It really did not hit me until we boarded the plane. Within a few minutes I begin to think out loud. Several questions came out of my mouth, one right after another, not leaving time for any responses. I took my husband's hands and looked at him and said: "honey what just happened? Did we just buy another home? Will our home sell within the 90 days allotted on the contract? What happens if it does not?" My husband was calm and said, "Baby everything is going to work out fine God did not bring us this far to leave us." He was so right everything about this relocation was orchestrated by something greater than us. It was our destiny to relocate to Georgia and now our faith had to sustain us.

After we arrived home our house went on the market right away. We were on a tight time schedule, and the only thing I kept saying was, I just want to be in our new home before the children began school in mid-August. In order to meet that timeline it was all predicated on the sale of our home in Illinois. I will never forget the day our realtor had scheduled the open house for the general public. It was on a Sunday afternoon and we experienced the most horrific weather on that day. It was rainy, windy and cool even for the Midwest it was bad.

My mom invited us over for Sunday dinner and in my mind I kept thinking, no one is going to be out on a day like today. This open house would definitely be a do over. The next day our realtor called and asked if he could stop by our home. He wanted to talk with us both together.

I thought this must be bad news. We had priced the house to sell maybe he thought we should lower the price, to get a quick sell based on our need to relocate to Georgia by August. When he arrived we all sat at the kitchen table beginning with a little small talk. I kept thinking just blurt it out already what happened at the open house yesterday?

Our realtor began the conversation and said, "In all of my twenty-five plus years as a realtor I have never experienced such a successful open house in the midst of such severe weather conditions. Families just kept coming and I have three offers to present. Two are very strong so I will present those both to you and give my recommendation." I knew God had orchestrated the entire day as a test of our faith to trust him completely and not to put our confidence in what we see. A sunny warm day does not necessarily mean success in the sale of your home. Conditions on the outside may appear to be stormy and disastrous but God can work a miracle in the midst of a storm. Within two weeks on the market our home at 3215 Newcastle Road Waukegan, Illinois was sold.

It was official, in August 1999 we packed up our entire family, along with all of our possessions and off to Georgia we drove. After thirteen hours in the car we reached our new destination. I drove one car with our teenage son and my husband drove the other car with our middle school daughter.

Due to the fact our house sold so quickly, once we arrived in Georgia we had to stay in a hotel for two weeks. During this time the final touches were being put on our new home. Three days before the first day of school started, we were nestled into our beds in our new home. All of our prayers had been answered!

***

CHAPTER 8

THE "PEACH" STATE OF MIND

During the first few years of relocating to Georgia our entire family went through a period of adjustment. We all had to make new friends, find a new place of worship, adjust to the traffic, and identify new places to shop. Most important I had to learn how to navigate all of the Peachtree streets in the Atlanta metro area. Our children especially our daughter had difficulty in making adjustments to the new school environment. I guess we never truly thought about the fact that their first day of school would be a frightening experience. Riding a bus where you do not know one single student is difficult and challenging at best. My husband was the only person in the family that had something familiar to him and that was his IT position. He had been with the company for fourteen years. All of his colleagues were yet interacting with him daily, remotely versus face-to-face. In order to assist the family get acclimated to our new environment, the first year I was blessed to do volunteer work at their schools respectively. Decorating our new home was also a wonderful experience.

In 2000 I secured a position at a not-for-profit organization that would become a very important part of our sustainability over the next thirteen years. Life was going extremely well.

Our children had settled in and made new friends. My husband continued to get promotions on his job and my career was advancing. I worked outside the home because I wanted to work not because I had to and this felt good! We lived primarily off of my husband's income and saved the majority of my income.

Over the next three years from 2000-2003 I increased our savings plan. We took family vacations every year, we had no credit card debt and our credit rating was excellent. Everything we purchased was cash and carry.

If we made a credit card transaction we would pay the bill in full within 30 days as to not accrue any interest. It felt so good to have discretionary money and what gave me the most joy was to have my mom on a monthly stipend. She never asked us for a dime but she had always been our biggest fan from day one.

I remember our very first home purchased in 1986 a modest bungalow built in the 30's with the original woodwork and a one car garage.

Arrangements had been made to secure the closing cost funding needed to purchase our first home; but the agreement fell through just a few days prior to our closing date.

We were young I was 25 and my husband was 28. We always tried to be self-sufficient and did not want to ask anyone to assist us but we needed mom's help.

My mom loaned us the money in order to close on our home without any questions asked. We paid her back in full within two weeks. The fact that mom trusted us let us know she loved us unconditionally. We will never forget her unselfish love toward us throughout our entire marriage.

My husband has always practiced God first, our family second and he was third. He would always tell me as long as you and the children are cared for I am good. He never ceased to surprise me with romantic weekends: An intimate candlelight dinner with my favorite foods and a bubble bath trimmed with lighted candles in our jetted tub after a long hard day in the office. Yes he spoiled me royally and I spoiled him right back. It gave me joy to surprise him with birthday weekends at a special hotel; preparing his favorite meals and desserts all homemade of course; serving him in bed and running his bubble bath after a hard day at work.

One of my most memorable birthdays I experienced was in November of 2000. It was my 40th birthday and my husband celebrated my birthday for an entire week! Each day I would wake up there would be a gift on our bathroom counter. He gave me items that I would not necessarily purchase for myself; not that I did not deserve them I was somewhat frugal and wanted to make sure all of my purchases were meaningful not just emotional shopping. (I am so over that now! Bring it on...)

The first day of my week long 40th birthday celebration began with Victoria Secret shall I say more..., the second day a coach purse, the third day a beautiful coach wallet to go with the purse, the fourth day gift cards to all of my favorite stores Macy's, TJ Maxx and Marshalls. My motto is: it is not where you shop but how you put it together that makes the fashion statement. The fifth day a goodie bag with all of my favorites including chocolate pecan caramel turtles. Delightful is what comes to my mind when I think of those chocolates. The sixth day he presented me with tickets to a musical at the Fox Theatre in Atlanta which would also include dinner.

The tickets to the musical that were presented on the sixth day were to be used on the seventh day of the birthday celebration. I was all dressed and ready to go out on our date night. My sweet hubby told me he had to step out for a few moments. I thought he was going to get gas. It seemed to take him longer than usual to return. I was getting anxious and did not want to miss the curtain call. Nothing worse than arriving late to a musical and stepping over folks! I actually begin to get a little attitude and I thought if we are late…He should have purchased gas earlier today he had all day.

Finally I heard the garage door open so I ran downstairs to meet him and as the garage door reached the top I noticed he arrived in a 1999 E320 Silver Mercedes Benz.

I thought, oh bless his heart he rented a car for our evening. So he got out of the car opened my door and I sat down on the passenger side smiling. I said to him, "So you rented a car so we could go to the Fox Theatre in style?" His response was "No I did not rent a car, Happy Birthday sweetheart." I almost hyperventilated I just kept saying, "What! How did you swing this? Is it really mine? Can we afford this car? You see as stated earlier I always managed the finances so I knew if there were any large sums of cash withdrawn from our joint account. Had I missed something? He said no worries I have been working on your birthday for a year and I am so glad I pulled it off. After that I sat back and enjoyed my new car with the best date I ever had.

So if you have not caught on by now my husband is my best friend, the love of my life, an outstanding husband and father of our two children. His generosity and gift of helping others is not limited to his immediate family but to our house of worship and community at large. He was the recipient of the Community Service Award given by the Georgia Legislative Black Caucus. I share some of his accolades not to boast but to share with you some of his cherished attributes. These attributes are a tribute to his character. He is an amazing man that has lived out his faith and walked with integrity. He has always provided for his family through hard work and dedication. I remember him sharing with me early in our marriage, that he wanted to transition out of the retail business to increase his career opportunities. He wanted to stabilize his work schedule, allocating more time to be with the family. It was always about the betterment of the family. He had diligently climbed the corporate ladder for twenty-two years.

Who would have ever expected he would be downsized three times over the next ten years; and in 2008 it lasted two years and three months. During this time our love for God and each other would be tested. Would we survive or thrive through economic uncertainty? Would our faith and love be enough to sustain us? Only time would tell!

***

MORE THAN A PAYCHECK

CHAPTER 9

LIVING A DOWNSIZED LIFE

According to 2014 Merriam-Webster, Inc. an online site: down-size means, 1. "To reduce in size; especially to design or produce in smaller size. 2. To fire (employees) for the purpose of downsizing: to undergo a reduction in size."

In other words, to be "downsized" allowed an employer to trim the high waged earners. Employers can then go back and update a job description and repost the business need for 50% of the cost. It is a win-win for the company...not so much for the employee who no longer has a way to care for their family.

The majority of the nation began to experience the economic turndown in 2007. High unemployment rates and stagnant growth in the economy impacted my husband three times beginning in 2003.

The Tornado:

Throughout our marriage we have always tried to be transparent. So...I knew the insurance company, for which my husband had been employed for seventeen years, was going through some organizational changes.

However never in a million years did I think we would be faced with my husband losing his livelihood. I remember it like it was yesterday. My husband Maurice affectionately called "Sweet Reese" called me into our bedroom. He sat me on his lap and said, "Honey I have something I need to share with you; the company I currently work for, is doing some re-organization changes and telecommuting will no longer be extended as a work option. All employees will need to interview for their current position and those positions are located in Illinois." My head was spinning and multiple questions and statements were racing through my mind.

Did this mean we would have to place our home in Georgia on the market? Return to Waukegan, Illinois in order to find another home comparable in price? Homes in the Midwest were more expensive. To purchase a home compatible would be an added expense long term.

There were just too many questions to be answered and so little time. We had been given two options: 1. Return to Illinois and have my husband interview for a position, for which there were no guarantees; and have our family uprooted or 2. Accept the package being offered and remain in Georgia.

After I got over the shock of it all we prayed together. We both agreed it would be easier for my husband to find another career opportunity in Georgia. To uproot our entire family, sell our home in Georgia, without any guarantees of employment in Illinois, was no longer an option. I had peace about our decision, even though uncertainty did surround me on the inside.

We called the children into the room and my husband shared with them what was going on. Their only concern was did we have enough money to remain in our house, pay the bills and buy groceries.

We assured them both that we were not going to be homeless. Children always have a funny way of bringing things into prospective. What was most important was the ability to meet our basic human needs. Whatever we faced we would do it as a family.

The first time my husband was downsized, it lasted one year from 2003-2004. Our entire family was in transition. I immediately went to my employer and added the family onto my health insurance plan. My husband secured additional certifications to make him more marketable in the IT field. Our daughter, Christine was transitioning into her freshman year in high school. Our son, James had recently graduated from high school. He was a college freshman at Georgia Southwestern State University in Americus, GA. We were able to pay cash for our son's first year in college. We did not want him to acquire student loan debt as we did while in college. Financial planners would not recommend this due to our financial transition status. However as a parent, you always want to see your children do better financially and keeping him out of debt was our goal.

Living within our financial means, not accruing credit card debt, and our existing savings, helped to sustain us. The financial package deal from my husband's employer reduced the impact of my husband being downsized. This of course was strictly from a financial containment perspective. The emotional impact of my husband losing his job and career status after seventeen years was real. It had to be impactful to no longer have means to financially provide for our family. He never communicated the loss to me verbally. What I closely observed regarding my husband's attitude and behavior, was he maintained a positive outlook on life.

He made his job search a full time job. He threw himself into volunteer work in the community and at church to keep busy. This was his personal way of dealing with the loss. It is also a positive way to ward off becoming depressed. According to an article on cluewagon.com losing your job can be similar to losing someone you love. There is the immediate financial and social loss. Elisabeth Kübler-Ross an American Psychiatrist is known for her theory on the five distinct stages of grief. These five stages can also be used to describe grief as a result of a job loss:

1. Denial: This can't be happening to me? I have been a dedicated loyal employee.

2. Anger: How could they be doing this to me? Feeling betrayed by management.

3. Bargaining: Maybe if I just...we should have stayed in Illinois I would still be employed.

4. Depression: I'm never going to get a job. Ageism is real how do I get around it?

5. Acceptance: "It's going to be ok." Move on; better opportunities will come our way.

The facts were he was a committed, loyal, high achiever who trained other IT professionals on the team. He had experienced a stellar career with this company receiving awards and earning a substantial salary while building his 401K. The bottom line was this was a business decision made in order to meet the business needs of the organization. Bad things do happen to good people it is how you handle what happens that makes the difference.

After being home for a year in 2004 my husband secured a contract position with a major corporation. This was a totally new way at looking at employment for him. He had to negotiate the hourly rate which was usually a higher rate than being a salaried employee however he had to purchase his own benefits. There are minimal fringe benefits sick leave, vacation, and bereavement. In most cases if you do not work you do not get paid. I really did not care about the benefits so much because regardless of what happened with our careers; we always kept a separate life insurance policy. I also continued to maintain the medical and dental benefits with my employer for the family. This was a new responsibility for me and I was glad to contribute. My husband was on a twelve month assignment however after six months on the job he decided to leave to accept a full time offer that extended full benefits.

He had always had full time jobs with full benefits 401K, medical, dental, life insurance, vacation, sick, holiday leave and access to bonus pay. When he initially told me he was accepting the full time position I was excited. Given his experience in IT; I knew it should be comparable or at least within the $10K range. I was wrong on both counts it was a $30K salary reduction and that was the beginning of our loss in wages over the next several years.

After completing one year of college our son decided to go into the US Navy so in 2004 we no longer had to subsidize tuition for him. Our daughter graduated from high school in 2006 and was accepted to attend the University of Georgia (UGA). She earned the "Hope" scholarship that covered her tuition so we just needed to subsidize housing and dining commons cost along with incidentals.

After her freshman year she moved off campus into an apartment so we had to budget monthly rental payments for that. Our goal was to maintain our household while keeping her out of student loan debt. Although my husband took a huge salary reduction I continued to advance in my career resulting in three promotions and salary increases. This could have not come at a better time. It seemed like we were getting back on track slowly but surely or so I thought?

The Tsunami:

Could I finally take a deep breath? It had been four years since my husband had been downsized. He had been working as an IT professional within a financial corporation and their stability as a company seemed to be okay. Even though our combined income had taken a hit from the initial downsizing we adjusted and continued to live within our means. The second and most severe downsizing happened in 2008. I refer to it as our personal tsunami. It hit fast, hard, and the financial impact had long lasting implications to our savings and retirement. We are still rebuilding from the turbulence today!

It was mid-morning in 2008 and my office telephone rang. As I glanced at caller ID I noticed it was my husband. Responding cheerfully to his calls there was a certain tone in his voice that sounded serious and he said, "honey my job has been impacted. Human Resources told me a few moments ago and I must leave the premises within the next thirty minutes."

I could not believe what I was hearing, thoughts begin racing through my mind. Thoughts like is there a severance because he had only been there for four years. There was a severance it was very small. All I wanted to do at this point was to encourage him and support him. I responded, "Honey it will be ok." After I hung up the phone I thought will it really be ok?

We were in the thick of a recession and opportunities were diminishing. My only thought was to be by his side and I wanted to go home to support him.

So I met with the Director of our Division and shared with her that I needed to leave for the day. On the way home I stopped at the grocery store and purchased his favorite foods and went home to prepare the best meal ever.

When I arrived home he was in relatively good spirits and said, honey you did not have to come home and my response was I know but I wanted to be with you!

I prepared some comfort foods and we agreed we would be in this together. We had no idea the entire world was truly in the thick of a brutal economic turndown. The financial company he worked for had outsourced all of the positions to India leaving a skeleton team to train the new hires.

Our family dynamics were different than the initial downsizing in 2003. We had a daughter at the University of Georgia that needed financial support. My salary just barely covered our expenses and we would have to subsidize with our savings. Medical insurance for the family had increased so every dollar was accounted for. Each month I had to transfer money from our savings account to the checking's to ensure bills were paid on time. Looking back I am just grateful we had the money saved. Many families did not have adequate savings and as a result would lose their homes to foreclosure. The heartbreaking moment came when we had to share with our daughter she would have to take out student loans to complete the final two years of college.

I had to co-sign her student loans something that I said I would never do after paying our loans back but we did not want her to miss an opportunity to earn her college degree. This was an investment into her future.

This was never the plan as we wanted to give our children a start in life debt free however we had to maintain our home and day-to-day expenses. She was quite the trooper and we are confident with

God's help we will help her pay those student loans back 100%.

Where is the Sun?

This was the third downsizing that we experienced within a ten year range.

The impact of this downsizing was unique in that in May of 2013 after 13 years in my role at a not-for-profit organization I was no longer employed in that capacity. I did receive a package that helped to sustain us as we were both home unemployed together for four months.

This had never been our experience in 35 years of marriage. One of us always had a job and I can tell you with no uncertainty it took our faith, our established friendship and the ability to pursue and create fun to remind us this was only a season.

We experienced so many miracles and open door opportunities that kept us afloat through this transitional time in our lives. We had to remind ourselves that God was our source and not our skill-set or capabilities. God has never failed us yet! My husband has continued to work as an IT professional and I support him in that role.

The combined duration of the three downsizings lasted a total of almost four years over a ten year period. None of which were attributed to him quitting or being terminated but were solely based on a business decision of the organization to downsize. When you put that in perspective my husband has worked 31 of the 35 years of marriage providing for our family.

However those four years were at a pivotal time in our lives that would test our relationship in the areas of my husband's net worth, role reversal, communication, emotional impact, intimacy, and support network. I will expand on all of these areas and provide tips that can be used to overcome the obstacles in later chapters.

I believe the lesson I had to learn was God used my husband as a resource or steward to provide for our family. My husband was not my sole source. God is and has always been our provider.

CHAPTER 10

HE'S WORTH WHAT???

If my husband is defined by who he is and not by what he does or what he makes, what is his net worth? According to Wikipedia "Net worth is the total assets minus total liabilities of an individual or company". When I think of the word asset, I think of something or someone who adds value. When I think of a liability, I think of something that hinders or takes away from my quality of life.

Society will place a value on ones standing in the world by establishing social classes based upon income earning levels.

When tangible income has been taken out of your household, what qualities and characteristics define your spouse? If there was no paycheck, would your husband still have value?

Net worth within a marriage is not solely monetary. It was my husband's character that gave me strength, when he was no longer employed receiving a paycheck. For me those characteristics that contributed to his net worth included the following:

- Demonstrated faith in God – Never wavered that God had a greater plan for him.
- Love for his family – Willing to do whatever it takes to provide for his family.
- Character – Continued to carry himself as a consummate professional during adversity.
- Integrity – Never compromised his beliefs to obtain material gain.

- Perseverance – Continued to pursue career opportunities for over two years consistently and daily even in the face of constant rejection.
- Volunteerism – Continued to give back to the community, not-for-profits and his House of Worship during the time of transition.

My husband's net worth far exceeded his paycheck and helped to put things in perspective for me. Do not get me wrong, the ability to generate revenue for our family and home are important. Adequate finances contribute to the bottom line in reducing debt, and contribute to a quality of life. A paycheck however, was not the only attribute my husband had to offer me. His ability to generate income certainly did not define his total net worth. What defines your husband? Who is he beyond his career or skill-set? What characteristics or contributions does he make in the world?

Could you honestly respond or be willing to have a candid conversation regarding the following questions?

1. How would you react if your husband was downsized today without any prior warning?

2. What if your husband could no longer make a financial contribution to the family that lasted more than six months?

3. How would you introduce your husband to your colleagues at a business function if he had been unemployed more than one year?

4. Do you continue to hold your husband in high regard to family and friends?

5. What would your response be at a social gathering if asked so…What does your husband do for a living?

I encourage you to be proactive. Make a list of your husband's attributes that define who he is in the face of adversity.

The list can remind you of his net worth. The list will also prepare you to have appropriate public responses to questions related to his career. These questions may put you in an awkward and uncomfortable situation if not prepared. I know, because I experienced and lived through these questions during times while my husband was downsized.

CHAPTER 11

BUSINESS AS USUAL? NOT...

According to the Bureau of Labor statistics with more than 5.5 million Americans unemployed for twenty-seven weeks or longer the rule of thumb of having three to six months' worth of income saved for expenses may not be enough.

Financial experts recommend putting aside at least nine months to a year of income in an emergency account. An example of this is: If it takes $5,000 per month to manage your home you should have $30,000 as a six month emergency fund or $60,000 set aside as a contingency plan if you are laid off work for one year. This would be the optimal goal to strive for but the reality is how many of us honestly can say we have an emergency fund to meet a one year job loss. According to Gail Cunningham, spokeswoman for the National Foundation for Credit Counseling in Washington, DC, "people are often out of work as long as nine months, and if they don't have savings they live on credit. As a result even when a job is secured they are behind because now there is debt to repay." Does this sound familiar to anyone out there?

As stated earlier we have always tried to live within our means and yes initially we were those people who had saved 10-20% of wages earned per pay period and had a substantial savings account that sustained us for two years.

After my husband experienced the second downsizing that lasted two years and three months, we exhausted our emergency fund and 401K to survive. During this time period we experienced unforeseen medical emergencies, and surgeries that required medical co-pays, along with routine car and home repairs.

We were now the family living paycheck to paycheck. This was unfamiliar territory for us. Normally, I had a backup plan... As a woman, did I experience fear, frustration, and thoughts of, will this ever end? You bet!!! Our faith in God however never wavered. In the midst of this storm we never stop giving 10% for tithes and offerings.

Some folks could not understand the principle of tithing. In their mind we should have reduced our credit card debt with tithe and offering money. Let me explain, that there is absolutely no doubt in my mind, that giving our tithe and offering even during difficult times helped to sustained us. We never missed a mortgage payment and none of our monthly bills were ever paid late. This had to be a supernatural move of God on our behalf.

Debts incurred must be paid off and we are committed both ethically and morally to pay all debts made. Our confidence is that the principle of seedtime and harvest will work! According to Genesis 8:22 (KJV), *"While the earth remaineth, seedtime and harvest, and cold and heat, and summer and winter, and day and night shall never cease."* With God's help, we will be financially whole and debt free.

Now some of you may be asking how do you plan to become financially debt free? My husband and I created an action plan that includes generating additional revenue; continuing to sow tithes and offerings, and to allocate monthly payments to our outstanding creditors systematically until paid in full. I recommend sitting with your spouse and take a real look at your finances both income and expenses. Create an immediate realistic budget plan that meets your needs. These are some of the actions we took to jump start our plan and to move us forward. I hope these tips can be used as tools to get you started:

Helpful Tips!

1. Tithes: If you tithe continue this principle by giving 10% of your income.

2. Establish a savings: the goal is to save something $10.00 per week is $520.00 saved in a year. Increase your savings amount as debts are paid. Target 5-10% of take home income as an ultimate goal per pay period. This is the "pay yourself first plan".

3. Create a Budget Journal: Begin by listing all income and expenses. Get a clear picture where you stand financially. What is your status? Are you operating in a surplus, break even or in a deficit? (Use this list as a tool to create a working realistic monthly budget)

4. Decrease monthly utility bills: (Cable, telephone, electric, gas) Call the utility company and secure competitive rates. The gas and electric companies will always give a competitive rate and fixed rates. This is no time for loyalty; use the utility that will provide the best rate. The ultimate goal is to reduce monthly spending.

5. Contact your creditors: Contact creditors immediately and advise of loss of income as a result of your husband being downsized. Request possible financial accommodations such as: unemployment hardship deferments or reduction in interest rates. Most creditors will be accommodating. Be proactive, this may help protect your credit rating if this is a concern. Do not bury your bills in a drawer wishing they will go away, they do not.

6. Identify quick wins: Target credit card debt with the lowest balance and high interest rates and pay that account off first. This will allow you to experience "a win" in debt reduction. (Do not become overwhelmed or discouraged; debt reduction takes time, consistency, diligence and perseverance.)

7. Prepare meals at home: Prepare a weekly menu, purchase ingredients based upon your menu for the week. Stay away from the money gobbler of junk food. Take your lunch to work at least four days per week. This is great way to stabilize spending and contributes to a healthy lifestyle.

8. If you would like to treat yourself and eat out one time per week and it is a cash transaction, within the budget do so. If eating out is not in the budget, be creative and prepare your meals

at home. Eating nutritious home cooked meals is healthier.

9. Generate Revenue: Gifts and talents can mean cash flow. Is there something that you do with ease that you can get paid for? Have family and friends told you I would pay you to... Sit down and draft a list of your strengths. One or more of those strengths may generate extra income.

The extra money can contribute toward reducing the household debt. Just remember you are not alone. There is no shame in starting over. Debt did not accrue overnight, and it will take time to become debt free. Make a plan; it is the first step to succeeding.

***

CHAPTER 12

BRINGING HOME THE BACON

As mentioned in Chapter 8 the "Downsized" chapter, the longest duration my husband had been impacted by unemployment began in 2008 and ended in 2010. Two years and three months to be exact.

During this time period, my role as the Director of the Careers Division at a not-for-profit organization continued to flourish. The government invested millions of dollars to fund, on-the-job training programs and extended unemployment benefits to the prolonged unemployed. Our goal was to get people back to work by any means necessary, especially those dislocated workers. My husband was considered a dislocated worker, for the first time in his career.

Not many of my colleagues knew my husband had been impacted the first year. It was not my habit to share my personal business in the work place. I did however know the power and importance of networking. So during year two of him being downsized I networked constantly on his behalf. All of our combined efforts seemed to be ineffective. Recruiters were not calling and interviews were not being scheduled. The IT jobs had dried up. Employers were hiring a new workforce for less pay, who resided in other countries. The overall job loss in the United States was substantial.

In reflection, several questions came to my mind such as: What was God's plan for our lives? What lessons should we be learning from all of this? To be transparent, the life lesson was simple but not easy to digest. God wanted me to truly understand. My husband was the conduit or tool God used throughout our marriage to provide. However God was, and always will be, our source of provision.

My husband had always been the primary bread winner in our home and suddenly our financial roles were reversed. Along with my new role came the responsibility of paying for the medical, dental, life insurance and 401K as deducted from my diminishing paycheck.

The ability to contribute and help sustain our family, during these turbulent times, gave me a sense of accomplishment. Along with the new responsibility came a new type of pressure. No longer did I have the luxury to work because I wanted to; but I worked to keep our family afloat. During that time period 2007 forward the entire country had been hit by the economic decline.

Massive layoffs, home foreclosures, and double digit unemployment rates were being experienced across the country especially here in Georgia. As challenged as we were in our reduction in finances, it could have been a lot worse. Many families lost tangible items such as: their homes and became homeless; 401K balances were wiped out; savings accounts dried up; cars were repossessed; and other items of value. Others experienced, diminished self-esteem, severe depression, became suicidal and marriages were dissolved ending in divorce.

Several colleagues, friends and relatives wanted to know how I was able to maintain a positive outlook on life and maintain a healthy marriage during the financial role reversal time period.

Trust me I had days where I felt discouraged. Would this season in our lives ever come to an end? Some days I resented that a great position had not come through for my hard working husband; angry that other men with less IT experience than my husband were still working; and tearful that we lacked funds to pay for basic human needs. I asked myself the rhetorical question, "Why Us?" My husband always responds, "Why Not Us?" This experience was a life lesson. We were given an opportunity to make a positive impact on other marriages, as we lived out our faith during economic uncertainty. If our marriage could thrive during financial difficulty, theirs could too!

Extended unemployment for a man and the inability to provide for his family, can impact every area of the relationship. These areas include communication, intimacy, self-esteem, and self-worth.

Each couple may react differently depending upon the foundation of the marriage. I was curious as to how other wives handled their relationship when their husband had been downsized.

It was interesting to actually interview several wives from diverse demographic backgrounds in order to secure their candid responses. What tools did they use to overcome each obstacle when their husband had been downsized six months or more?

Interview #1

Ethnicity: *African American*

Age demographic: *Over 60*

How long have you been married? *42 years*

Has your husband ever been downsized? *Yes*

How long was your husband unemployed? 3 years

What Industry did your husband work? *Military and Civil Service Account Tech 15+ years*

Did you have enough savings to meet your day to day expenses: Yes or No? *No*

Did you have to use credit cards? *Yes*

Other Subsidies: *Subsidized income through military assistance as a result of being a veteran.*

Question: What was the biggest impact on your marriage?

Answer: *Lack of financial security impacted our communications and intimacy:*

Question: How did you address your challenges?

Answer: *When you look into your husband's eyes and know he is doing his best I began to focus on what really matters.*

We invested time together that included low cost activities. We prepared and cooked the majority of our meals at home. Reduced outside activities that required money we did not have to spend. We would go and purchase ice cream cones, go for walks, car rides, looked at houses and dreamed. To dream gave us hope that, this too shall past. We eventually came full circle built our dream home, paid off our debt and mortgage and now mentoring other young couples that they too can survive financial hardship.

Are you still married? *Yes and we are thriving. We look forward to celebrating 44 years of marriage in the summer of 2017.*

Interview #2

Ethnicity: *Caucasian*

Age demographic: *50-60*

How long have you been married? *30-40 years*

Has your husband ever been downsized? *Yes*

How long? *6-12 months*

What Industry did your husband work? *Insurance: Executive Level 15+ years*

Did you have enough savings to meet your day to day expenses? *Yes*

Did you have to use credit cards? *No*

Subsidized income through any external programs? *Unemployment Benefits*

Question: What was the biggest impact on your marriage?

Answer: *The unemployment impacted our communications, finances, and intimacy all areas of our marriage were impacted. We were fortunate to have severance, and unemployment to stabilize our day to day living.*

Question: How did you address your challenges?

Answer: *We removed the children from costly activities to free activities. The unknown was the terrifying. We clung to each other. When I think about it; it was the best time in our marriage. Our basic shopping methods changed we went from "name brand" shopping to purchasing "generic" brands. Entertainment was impacted drastically but we continued to do a few cheaper activities. This helped to maintain a sense of normalcy for* *our children who were age 2 and age 5. We seem to pull together on the big things!*

Are you still married? *Yes our relationship is strong and we are financially solid at this time.*

~*~*~*

Interview #3

Ethnicity: African American

Age demographic: *40-50*

How long have you been married? *24 years*

Has your husband ever been downsized? *Yes*

How long? *Over 2 years*

What Industry did your husband work? *Hospitality Management 13yrs 6 months*

Did you have enough savings to meet your day to day expenses? *Yes*

Did you have to use credit cards? *Yes*

Subsidized income through any other external programs? *No*

Question: What was the biggest impact?

Answer: *The prolonged unemployment impacted our ability to communicate. Initially I began to internalize things. My goal was to protect my husband's emotions, since he was no longer able to provide. Huge Mistake! Financially, I would physically get a headache every month when it was time to do the monthly bills, knowing there was a shortfall of money to meet our living expenses. We continued with intimacy physically but emotionally I was not there. At my breaking point I attribute our marriage surviving to the qualities of my husband. His ability to get me to open up and share my frustration, fears and stressors helped to move our relationship forward. I begin to open up and share my fears and he was able to comfort me* *and even though our situation may not have changed immediately I knew he was doing his best and had my back. As a God-fearing man who lives his faith daily his qualities were worth staying in the marriage. I value him as a person he is funny, outgoing, warm, kind, generous, a great listener, an awesome husband and father. Our faith along with these qualities got us through some extremely dark days. These qualities, not money or resources got us through and each day gets better.*

Are you still married? *Yes*

We are still working towards getting financially healthy. My husband returned to school and learned a new trade and I am excited to share he is gainfully employed.

Interview #4

Ethnicity: *Caucasian*

Age demographic: *50-60*

How long have you been married? *20-30 years*

Has your husband ever been downsized? *Yes*

How long was your husband unemployed? *1-6 months (Still Unemployed)*

What Industry did your husband work? *IT*

Did you have enough savings to meet your day to day expenses? *YES*

Did you have to use credit cards? *No (Not yet hopefully will not have to)*

Other Subsidies: *Severance package and bonus received from prior employer helped to meet day to day expenses. Will apply for unemployment compensation if need to do so.*

Question: What was the biggest impact on your marriage?

Answer: *Stress and trying to keep a positive light on things.*

Question: How did you address your challenges?

Answer: *Try to remain positive and not harp on things. I don't argue when he tells me that he's doing all he can. I do make recommendations though when I feel there's room for improvement in his methods of job hunting. The worse thing is addressing the clear discrimination against 50+ year-olds and/for those who are here on H1B visas and work at a reduced pay rate.*

Are you still married? *Yes*

The one saving grace is that we have become more religious and less focused on monetary things as we've gotten older. It makes it much easier with no children at home.

After interviewing these four women who represent wives from different ethnicities, income brackets and marital longevity there seemed to be one common thread that resonated throughout our conversation and that was, "communication" is the key in resolving all marital conflicts. They all seem to reflect upon what really matters those intangibles of character integrity, trust, respect and love.

These attributes cannot be purchased with cash or a credit card. When a spouse shuts down verbally and emotionally, it limits and stops the ability to move forward in finding solutions. Therefore, communication needs to take place around financial, intimacy and family matters. It is ok to feel frighten, and not have all of the answers when experiencing financial challenges but the key is to have the freedom to share those emotions in a safe environment without blaming. This leads nicely into the next chapter when I share communication styles from a male and female perspective along with verbal and non-verbal communication styles.

MORE THAN A PAYCHECK

CHAPTER 13

TALK TO ME!

The ability to communicate effectively is a key ingredient in all relationships. We underestimate the power of verbal and non-verbal communication skills. How they impact the atmosphere we create in our home. Most of my intimate friends would describe me as an extrovert. Probably 90% of the time I would definitely agree. In short I rarely meet a stranger. However I do have down times that I enjoy solitude and being alone. As a speech communications major and being on the forensics team in college I spent a lot of time honing my speaking skills. I am usually an upbeat, jubilant, joyous person who tries to find joy in any given situation. My sweet husband is a business administration major. Much of his IT career has been spent utilizing his independent problem solving and critical thinking skills. He is a combination of an extrovert and introvert personality type or 50% both personality types. He has a demeanor of calm and likes to think things thoroughly through, before actually responding.

Given our different personality types, this proved to be tricky in our ability to communicate effectively. My main challenge was finding the right time to discuss important topics. The tone and body language we use can result in a loving, nurturing and protected atmosphere or one that is hostile, combative and unprotected. Have you ever been in a deep conversation with your hubby, felt he was not engaged in the conversation, and saying very few words? Well do not be discouraged, there really is scientific data that says women speak 20,000 words per day and men speak 7,000 per day. That means we speak 13,000 more words than our spouse per day! I joke with my husband from time to time when he is in his quiet reflective mood. I will say, "honey did you use your 7,000 words for the day?" I will usually get a smile, but at least it is a sign to let me know this might not be the best time to discuss a matter that is of high importance to me. That being said, in order to ensure you are engaged in strategic conversation and not being tuned out we have to target our words. Make sure we execute what is most important, in order to get a good well thought out response. I also must say timing is everything and this takes years of practice.

Discussing finances can be tricky, especially if your spouse has been unemployed for a long period of time. Your spouse may experience feelings of employer rejection, resulting in not feeling valued. The inability to provide for the family may also impact their self-esteem diminishing their worth. Communication and being transparent are key in order to work through financial lack in a marriage.

Using "I feel" statements focus on characteristics of how one feels versus the word "you" that is more accusatory and places blame. Listening skills are an absolute and practicing what you are going to say without emotion will help to avoid the pitfall of your spouse immediately shutting down. An example of using an "I feel" statement would be: I feel anxious when we do not have enough money to pay our bills every month. Versus saying, you do not have a job, so we cannot pay our bills every month. The "I feel" statement denotes we are in this together but there are times I feel afraid.

The "you" statement denotes, you are the reason for our current financial predicament and I am blaming you. Negative nonverbal body language such as: The folding of arms, shrugging of shoulders, grunting, deep breaths and rolling of eyes do not help facilitate positive conversation. These actions may be more demeaning to your spouse because it is dismissive behavior. The goal is to replace the negative nonverbal body language with positive nonverbal body language such as: positive facial expression, eye contact, open arms, nodding in agreement. Every day I continue to work on my communication skills both verbal and nonverbal. The simple statement, "I'm Sorry" always helps to diffuse inappropriate communications. Believe you me my sweet husband will call me out when I fall short and vice versa. Having quality conversations over quantity is most important.

During the time when my husband was unemployed, each day after entering our home, I wanted to hear every detail of his job search activity. It was as if an attorney was interrogating him. This built resentment because I was not approaching him in a tone that was respectful and supportive. When a time was selected to approach the subject I begin to share how it helped me to know the status of his job search. Knowing the status of his potential career opportunities helped me to support his job search efforts. As a result he began typing up the status of his employment opportunities. Together we reviewed the list at least twice each month. Even though he may not have received an offer right away, he was making things happen. In order for me to support him, he needed to talk to me, keep me in the loop and be transparent. Most men are open to discuss almost anything after a great intimacy encounter so take advantage of those moments. It is not always what you say but it is how you say it that brings either positive or negative results. If you are out there right now thinking my husband and I are not communicating, I encourage you to take action.

Launch your 21 day plan to help improve your communications by taking the following steps:

Step 1: Write down topics you would like to discuss.

Step 2: Prioritize their importance most men do not want you to come at them with a list of 10-20 topics they feel attacked. List the top three.

Step 3: Select the best time to discuss. (Hint: After an intimate encounter is a great opportunity)

Step 4: After you present your topic give him your full attention including, good eye contact, positive body language and proper tone. These all reflect support. He can now feel secure in his response. Something men rarely articulate but may experience when facing financial challenges in the marriage is fear. Men have been socialized not to show fear or be afraid. In Chapter 15 I discuss being his cheerleader. He needs encouragement.

<u>Step 5</u>: Develop a strong communication plan for your marriage: A plan that is loving, respectful, and honors each spouse.

The ability to effectively communicate will help you face any adversity you may encounter. We certainly have needed both the "calmness" of my husband and my "take action" attitude in our 35 years of marriage. A combination of our communication styles has been effective in moving us forward during turbulent times. Practice makes perfect so I encourage you to launch your 21 day to positive communications in your relationship today.

***

CHAPTER 14

MY HERO – I STILL NEED YOU

(Exclusive Husband Chapter)

Most men take pride and have a sense of accomplishment in the fact that they can financially provide for their family. This is true even if their wives work or shall I say this is true in our marriage. My husband would always tell me as long as you and the children are provided for financially I am happy and at peace.

When a man no longer can financially provide or contribute to the household his self-worth is attacked. He may question himself internally and ask the rhetorical question does my wife still need or desire me emotionally and sexually? How many times have you heard that men need sexual intimacy and women need security?

This is not to say that women do not enjoy sexual intimacy but the majority of us can agree that women are given to arousal when we feel financially secure. We like to know our financial obligations can adequately be paid each month. It is difficult to turn on romance at any given moment when your mortgage is at risk.

It is not conceivable to a man nor should it be to put their entire sexual intimacy on hold while he is unemployed. This behavior would be leaving the door open to infidelity. At the same time husbands will need to understand and be creative in building their spouses morale during this time of transition. As a result she will be open to continue nurturing the sexual intimacy in the marriage and not abort this important component. Sexual intimacy promotes oneness; to deviate or discontinue that role would leave a void. To become roommates passing in the night is a trap you want to avoid at all cost.

It was easy to fall into a rut of prolonging our intimate encounters. My husband communicated how important it was to know I still desired him sexually. Sharing his heart with me was a wakeup call and I became intentional to cultivate our intimacy. I never stopped loving him, I just got caught up in the daily grind of going to work, coming home making sure the children were okay, and surviving my own fears…When would he find a career opportunity again?

Listed below are some tools that may help a husband maintain a healthy relationship with their wife, as they navigate during turbulent times of financial uncertainty:

1. Build up her trust in you and help her feel secure. Share with her that this is only a season and together you are going to achieve financial security again.

2. Check in with her emotionally. Is she feeling overwhelmed, depressed, or anxious? Pray with her and praise her for carrying the financial responsibility for the family.

3. Lower your expectations in the home and take on additional responsibilities such as: prepare dinner, be proactive with household chores and yard work and prepare a bubble bath so when she arrives home she can relieve the workplace stress. Remember it is about effort not perfection. She will be so delighted of your kindness and as a result this will relax her and move you toward your need of a sexual encounter. A win-win for you both, she is emotionally engaged and you have an

opportunity to physically be one with her intimately. Your financial situation may not immediately change but you are building oneness and togetherness. Complimenting one another and creating a team effort versus being combative. My husband did all of these things and more while he was in career transition. I always felt loved and valued by his actions and his communications to me.

4. Keep your wife updated on your job search – This final tool is extremely important. Keep her engaged with your employer search progress. Communicate with her often, show her your employment job search records, your interview appointments so she can cheer you on and even ask her to do some mock interviewing with you. She will feel a part of the comeback plan.

Husbands you must know you are so very important during this financial transition in your marriage. Whatever creative things you can do to help build up your wife, help her feel secure, reminding her of the successes you have had in the past will move you both toward a brighter day. As I said before storms do not last forever cherish each day as a true present and a gift. As an assignment I would like each husband to make a list of the ways you can build morale in your wife and began to implement those activities over the next 21 days.

CHAPTER 15

CHEERLEADER

According to the Merriam-Webster's dictionary, "a cheerleader is a person who is a member of a group (typically a group of young women) who shout out special songs or chants to encourage the team and entertain the crowd during a game in sports like American football and basketball: a person who encourages other people to do or support something."

In review of the Omni Cheer blog posted November 3, 2014 written by Emily on www.omnicheer.com there are 18 qualities that describe a cheerleader that include the following:

- Focused
- Hard Working
- Tough
- Spirited
- Fit
- Determined
- Team Oriented
- Over-Achiever
- Multi-talented
- Proud
- Competitive
- Pressured
- Pumped
- Grateful
- Strong
- Committed
- Controlled
- All heart

I certainly did not know that my cheerleading skill-set would play such a major role in encouraging my husband, as well as myself during our economic decline. I had to use all 18 of the characteristics listed and then some to get through some difficult days.

As far back as I can remember I had always wanted to be a cheerleader. My favorite sports to cheer for was basketball and football. In my determination to prepare myself I set goals at the early age of eight. My weekly trips to the library included checking out books on cheerleading. In addition one of my childhood best friends who resided next door had a cousin who was very good in gymnastics. She taught us how to execute with precision the basic gymnastic moves; a cartwheel, round off, front jump, and the splits.

We would practice winter, spring, summer and fall. We mastered these gymnastic moves with great enthusiasm and excellence. In doing so cheerleading squads were formed in elementary school before even reaching the junior high school level. This was our opportunity to practice before official tryouts.

As a result of investing time in the early stages of my life I was able to compete and cheered for the basketball team in junior high school both 7th and 8th grade. Then upon entering high school after completing freshman year I made the sophomore squad culminating in varsity basketball and football cheerleading respectively. This eventually propelled me to try out at the college level eventually making the varsity basketball cheerleading squad.

During the early years of preparation cheering for both winning and losing teams helped me to use those same skills in my marriage. In reflection out of all of the years that I was a cheerleader not once did I quit the squad because of disappointment or of a team loss. I was committed and focused to the team and squad in spite of the outcomes.

During our engagement stage in our relationship we took divorce off the table which of course freed us from the threat of ever walking away from the marriage. Financial adversity and impact would not separate us so finding the appropriate tools to address concerns was of great importance. I needed to be able to pull from every resource possible to ensure my husband was whole and I was whole.

The cheerleading characteristic I align myself with the most is "All Heart". I knew my husband loved me, I knew all of the years he had been consistent and provided emotionally and financially for our family. This was my time to pay it forward to him and our relationship. Just like he had my back all of those years, he needed to know I had his back supporting his unforeseen job loss:

In my marriage I was committed to the covenant relationship which supersedes a contractual relationship. A contract is an agreement created by man and can be broken. A covenant is created by God and will last a lifetime. There were days that I did not feel focused, committed, enthusiastic, strong, all heart, etc.... Those were the days I had to push through my immediate feelings and use my faith to encourage and uplift my husband and myself. Words of affirmation like: We are going to make it; this is just a season; this too shall pass; no difficulty or storm last forever. The sun would shine again became my prayer, song and chant!

***

CHAPTER 16

RE-TOOLING THE ROMANCE

Once you have successfully motivated your spouse utilizing the cheerleading chapter as your guide; I would encourage each couple to come up with some romantic retooling tips to recharge your relationship. To assist you, I have included several romantic activities from actual couples that you may want to consider. The actual names have been changed to protect the identity of the couples.

#1 The bubble bath:

After an extremely long tiring day at work, I called my husband on the way home to share my frustration. Upon my arrival to my surprise a bubble bath awaited me. Love music was playing softly in the background and the atmosphere was calm. My husband actually bathed me and massaged my entire body. After the bath was over, we ate a wonderful dinner he had prepared. We danced to music until all of my tension and tiredness was gone. I am not going to tell you what happened next...

#2 Coupons of Love – No expiration date:

My husband created a coupon book with five coupons that could be redeemed at any time. Each coupon was decorated with colors of red, purple and pink. One was for kisses, one for a bubble bath, one for a home cooked meal, one for a massage and one for unlimited.... Well you get the point...

#3 Scavenger Hunt

After a long day at work my husband would have a scavenger hunt for me throughout the house with rose petals leading the way. Once I reached the final destination there awaited me a bubble bath, massage or a candlelight dinner. He also likes to shampoo my hair and paint my toenails which I find extremely romantic.

#4 Picnic after Dark

One of the most romantic dates I experienced, was a picnic under the stars. After we played tennis in our community my husband drove me to the park. Our favorite foods were hidden away in the trunk of the car in a picnic basket. He poured sparkling cider into two beautiful goblet glasses, our meal was complete. We enjoyed a picnic under the moonlight while beautiful love music played softly in the background.

These are just a few re-tooling tips that couples have used to help maintain a healthy relationship. The re-occurring theme is these activities did not require a lot of money. The couples have chosen to: Invest time, creativity, and set the atmosphere in order to foster a healthy relationship. Note: All of these romantic tips were initiated by the husbands.

CHAPTER 17

THE SUN WILL SHINE AGAIN

I wish I could tell you there was a perfect formula that would prevent your marriage from ever being impacted by medical hardship, job loss or financial lack but that simply is not true.

Regardless of your current financial status, or the amount of money you have saved "Life Happens!!!" True security in a relationship is not in the tangible things we can touch like our careers, homes, furniture, cars, and savings accounts. These things are important but can be taken away.

What would sustain your marriage if suddenly without any notice you had no income and your savings were at a zero balance? In my heart I knew it was the intangibles such as: Our faith in God, integrity, character, hope, confidence, trust, friendship, and love that allowed our marriage to thrive during financial adversity. I never knew how much I needed to pull from those intangibles to sustain our relationship until I was truly tested. We are still on the road to financial recovery but with our faith in God, commitment to each other, and a written plan to get out of debt we are confident we will walk in abundance, debt free.

Our goal is to give more to the ministry and pay it forward to others. Listed below are tools that I personally have used to assist our family during financial loss. They may help to safeguard your marriage during economic uncertainty.

Tools for Surviving Financial Loss:

1. Relinquish Your Pride: If you are like us and you have always worked and never asked for assistance, this is your first step and tool for survival. Remind yourself this is a season and once you are back on your feet you can pay it forward!

2. Home Owners: Programs vary from state to state but contact your mortgage company for possible deferment assistance to prevent foreclosure. Georgia had a HomeSafe mortgage assistance program that provides up to 18 months of mortgage payments directly to the lender. This program was designed to assist homeowners who are unemployed as a result of being downsized. Contact Housing and Urban Development (HUD) in your resident state.

3. Savings Account: If you managed to accumulate a savings use wisely. Withdraw

only what is needed to pay your month to month expenses while pursuing other income.

4. Limit or Stop going to the mall: If you go to the mall use it as a place to exercise, a walking trail only. This helps to maintain a healthy lifestyle and reduces stress. Leave your cash, debit and credit cards at home to avoid the temptation to do emotional shopping. You would be surprised how much you could rack up in credit card debt with the mindset that you are the primary bread winner and now all I do is work and carry the financial responsibility of the family. If it is not a "NEED" leave it there. A need is life sustaining. A Michael Kors purse, shoes or outfit is not. (Not that there is anything wrong with owning those items, it may just be delayed gratification at this time of financial transition)

5. Think Outside the Box: I confess I am a baby boomer. Baby boomers grew up with the mindset that we were married to our careers. If we did an outstanding job we would be there until we retired. When the economy tanked for everyone in the USA in 2007 many of the baby boomers were downsized, offered severance packages and found they were now unemployed. Baby boomers had to begin thinking outside the box. We no longer had the luxury to only focus on permanent full time positions. As employers continue to streamline the workforce, job seekers must be flexible. Contract assignments and entrepreneur opportunities were viable work options. You can purchase your medical, dental, 401K, and Life insurance with a staffing company just as you could if you were a full-time employee. The advantage of contract work is you usually make a higher salary. The disadvantage is the

contract assignments have an end date. In this economy nothing is promised and a full-time permanent position may have an end date you just do not know that up front, so go for it!

If your husband has acquired an expertise such as landscaping, minor house repairs, washing windows you may want to encourage him to use that skill-set to generate additional income; after all, the bottom line is to get paid.

6. Entertainment: Be creative, you must have and outlet individually and as a couple. All of these ideas are under $25.00 total. Most movie theaters offer a reduced rate if you attend the matinee usually before 4:00PM. The cost per ticket is $6.00 or less. Share popcorn or eat before you go. Make a picnic lunch and go to the park. If you reside in a community with amenities take advantage of the free tennis, swimming, and lake opportunities. Treat

yourself out to breakfast from time to time. The cost is usually cheaper than eating out for dinner.

7. Maintain an Intimate Connection: I saved this one for last because it may be the most important. Men value physical intimacy the ability to touch, feel and connect with their wife. Women value security and the ability to communicate: We like to use our 20,000 words a day without judgment, (I know...yes men only use 7,000 per day), we like to feel safe in our home and know the bills are being paid each month. While both physical intimacy and security are vital to the sustainability of a marriage. Both the husband and wife must take time out of the day to love and nurture the relationship. An important reminder, we are not competitors with our spouse but we complement one another. Your friendship and love will see you through difficult days. Once

you initiate intimacy, it truly builds your oneness and opens the door for transparency, communication and your husband's ability to share his heart freely.

These tools recommended to survive financial loss are shared out of my own experience. As you navigate through your own financial seasons, my hope and prayer is that you will integrate these tools into your marriage. The sun will definitely shine again in your relationship, before you know it, you will be on the road to recovery, and your marriage will no longer be in survival mode but it will be thriving!

CHAPTER 18

WHAT ARE PEOPLE SAYING... ENDORSEMENTS

"Wow where do I start...This book has inspired me in so many ways. It helped to remind me how important it is to marry your best friend. This book is for everyone...not just married couples. Once you begin reading, you won't put it down until you have finished it! I will be looking for the workbook, hopefully soon to come. "

Dena Parker
Controller
Round Lake, IL

***

A true story of love and commitment, Sharon Almon captures what women need to know about keeping your marriage fun when your money is funny. Best summed up with one line, "My husband's net worth far exceeded his paycheck and helped to put things in perspective for me", Sharon's personal story is a fabulous point of reflection for wives (and wives-to-be). And with money being a root of most failed marriages, it's time to take a serious look—Do you have the recipe to make it last forever? This no-fluff book offers insightful, engaging, encouraging, and real tips to weather your marriage during any financial storm. Don't let money (or the lack of it) change you.

Dr. Roz Ashford
Author, Personal Development Expert, & Talk Radio Host
Southern, USA

***

*"**More Than A Paycheck** is an amazing book for both wives and wives-to-be; a tool to help sustain marriages during financial upheavals! Sharon candidly and transparently shares the challenges she and her husband, Maurice, faced as their financial stability took a major turn. As a budget coach, I appreciate how Sharon provides financial tips to managing money wisely whether one is in a crisis or not. As we know, the number one topic of dispute in a marriage evolves around money issues. Sharon explains how wives and wives-to-be can confront and overcome the difficult economic times in their marriage. Thank you Sharon for obeying the Lord and sharing this much needed subject with your readers!"*

Kimberly Ivory Graves
Author of "Leaving Peace & Order"
Gurnee, IL

***

*"We are grateful to Sharon Almon for sharing her testimony and delivering insightful tools to help marriages survive financial adversities in this book, **More Than a Paycheck**.*

More Than a Paycheck *is a real life story, of real people and how their relationship survived financial difficulties. Regardless of where you are in your walk with Christ, this inspiring book helps you understand and translate into practical actions the multiple biblical principles in this matter.*

Maurice and Sharon Almon, who have been married for over 35 years, share life experiences and treasures in this book.

Eric and Nancy Montano
Spring of Life Couples Ministries
Atlanta, GA

***

"Sharon and Maurice are truly inspiring in their commitment to helping foster strong marriages. This book is both entertaining and educational. It will inspire you to find ways to support your spouse in hard times. Thank you, Sharon, for sharing this honest and upbeat story of living your faith through challenging times."

Dan Hayes
Executive Director of Atlanta Community Ministries &
Charlotte Hayes, M.A., L.P.C.
Career Counseling and Consulting
Atlanta, GA

***

MORE THAN A PAYCHECK

ABOUT THE AUTHOR

Sharon Almon's call has been to uplift, motivate, encourage and champion individuals particularly women who have counted themselves out. She considers herself a personal cheerleader and coach who have walked in her call and purpose through a career choice of working in the non-for-profit management arena for the past 15+ years. Sharon is a native of Illinois and relocated to the Atlanta metro area in 1999 with her wonderful husband Maurice of 35 years. Sharon and her husband were appointed marriage ministry coordinators in 2006 by Bishop Wiley Jackson. Motivating couples to invest in their marriage has been a joint passion. Strong marriages build strong communities. Couples are encouraged; that your marriage can thrive not just survive life challenges. The three keys to their successful marriage has been their faith, friendship and having fun. They have two adult children, James who has served in the US Navy for over 10 years and Christine a University of Georgia (UGA) graduate working in corporate America. Sharon enjoys gardening, crafts, cooking, traveling and entertaining.

To learn more about Sharon Almon visit: www.sharonlalmon.com

THE SUN WILL SHINE AGAIN

31440968R00117

Made in the USA
Columbia, SC
05 November 2018